M000076365

GHOSTLY
ENCOUNTERS

GHOSTLY ENCOUNTERS

CONFESSIONS OF A
PARANORMAL INVESTIGATOR

JEFF SCOTT COLE
WITH
JOHNATHON ROBSON

SKYHORSE PUBLISHING

For my son, Jakob;

Whether it's in the here and now or the hereafter,
I will always love you and be with you.

Disclaimer: This memoir is intended for education and entertainment. Although the author and publisher have made every effort to ensure that the information in this book was correct at press time, the author and publisher do not assume and hereby disclaim any liability to any party for any loss, damage, or disruption caused by errors or omissions. Some names and identifying details have been changed to protect the privacy of individuals.

Copyright © 2015 by Jeff Scott Cole and Johnathon Robson
All photos provided by authors, unless otherwise noted.

All rights reserved. No part of this book may be reproduced in any manner without the express written consent of the publisher, except in the case of brief excerpts in critical reviews or articles. All inquiries should be addressed to Skyhorse Publishing, 307 West 36th Street, 11th Floor, New York, NY 10018.
Skyhorse Publishing books may be purchased in bulk at special discounts for sales promotion, corporate gifts, fund-raising, or educational purposes. Special editions can also be created to specifications. For details, contact the Special Sales Department, Skyhorse Publishing, 307 West 36th Street, 11th Floor, New York, NY 10018 or info@skyhorsepublishing.com.
Skyhorse® and Skyhorse Publishing® are registered trademarks of Skyhorse Publishing, Inc.®, a Delaware corporation.
Visit our website at www.skyhorsepublishing.com.
10 9 8 7 6 5 4 3 2 1
Library of Congress Cataloging-in-Publication Data is available on file.

Cover design by Rain Saukas
Cover photo credit: Thinkstock

Print ISBN: 978-1-63220-584-1
Ebook ISBN: 978-1-63450-011-1

Printed in the United States of America

Acknowledgments

This book would not have been possible without the guidance and support of countless friends and family members, near and far. In particular, I would like to thank my editor Floyd Largent, who has been with me from the mammoths and mastodons of the early Paleo-Indian period, to the ghosts of the twenty-first century; my Literary Agent Carrie Pestritto of Prospect Agency, whose unwavering support, patience and friendship has been both anchor and buoy; and Skyhorse Publishing editor Nicole Frail, who saw the vision and believed in it. I thank my Dad, Herb and Judy, Bryan and Amy, Keith and Brenda, and most certainly the spirit of my dear mother Arlene, who I know keeps a watchful and protective eye on me, particularly when I step into dark creepy places. I thank my mentors and colleagues: Bruce Webb, Ralph Halse, Melissa Couch, and all my friends (faculty and former students) at Madison Local Schools in Ohio.

Additionally, Johnathon would like to thank his wife Sarah and Isaiah for their endless support during countless investigations, evidence review sessions, and the creation of *Ghostly Encounters*. He would also like to thank his parents Ruth, Max, and his sister Nancy for always being there and for encouraging his voyage into the paranormal field. Finally, we would like to express our deep thank to our C-Bus Paranormal team mates, current and past; Julie and Michael T., Doug "BJ" S., Christopher O., Andrew A., Mike H., and Ryan B. It has been a hell of a ride and the journey has only begun!

Table of Contents

Author's Note

‍

~~~~~~~~~~

Hi there, and thank you for selecting *Ghostly Encounters: Confessions of a Paranormal Investigator*. We are grateful and honored to be a part of your library. Before we serve up the entrée, allow us to offer appetizers we hope you will find technically and contextually helpful as you read through these pages and interact with this awesome technology.

Our intention was to create an interactive book, in print and digital formats, that will allow you to see and hear the bits and pieces of evidence we have collected from several recent investigations. Although the practical aspects of the investigations are straightforward as presented in the text, the form and nature of the evidence collected remains elusive. Why is one EVP (Electronic Voice Phenomenon) clear as a bell while another is a scarcely audible whisper? To be honest, we haven't a clue ... and neither does anyone else. Sure, there are tons of ideas, beliefs, theories, and sheer speculation, but nothing that answers this simple question with an equally simple answer.

With this in mind, we strongly recommend you use earbuds or headphones when listening to the attached video files and adjust the volume setting on your device accordingly. Some of the evidence is remarkably clear, requiring nothing more than your device's speaker; other bits are less obvious, especially when heard for the first time, and may require several replays. This is why all the evidence we have captured and included is repeated with subtitles. Though a few bits are a little challenging, trust us, they *are* there. And speaking of trust, let us consider this crucial subject.

What is trust, anyway? As a noun, trust is *reliance on the integrity, strength, ability, surety, etc., of a person or thing; confidence.* As a verb, trust is *to rely upon or place confidence in someone or something* (dictionary.com). Whether it's about your car or your friends, trust is about integrity and confidence—traits we both take very seriously. As we delve into the text and the chronology of investigations we have conducted, we hope that our honesty and candor warrant your respect and earn your trust.

Honesty and candor are also prime reasons why this book is subtitled as it is. In the reality TV/para-celebrity atmosphere that seems to have enveloped ghost hunting and paranormal investigating, both truths and troubling falsehoods, misunderstandings, and misinterpretations have emerged in what has truly become a pop culture phenomenon. The negative connotations confound and frustrate all paranormal investigators who take this field seriously . . . and yes, there are tens of thousands of us. This book is as much dedicated to them as it is to the curious enthusiast. It is remarkable how a few reality shows—some good, some bad—have influenced public understanding, perceptions, and even beliefs about paranormal phenomena. Certainly one of the best results of these programs is the awareness and intense curiosity they have raised in so many people. On the other hand, some programs have raised both eyebrows and questions in the paranormal investigating community as to the veracity of evidence presented and some of the methods and practices exhibited on television.

This being said, please understand that, besides this book, we are neither trying to sell you anything nor trying to convince you these phenomena are either real or imagined. That is for you to decide, though we think it is reasonable to assume (given the fact that you purchased this book) that you are at least curious about ghosts and spirits, even if you are not an experienced paranormal investigator with your own experiences.

This leads us to the context and *voice* of this book. Although we have both worked equally and extensively on all aspects of this project, an easily defined division of labor surfaced: Jeff wrote it, and John contributed to the writing and "tech'd" it, creating the clips, QR codes, storage for those links, and so on. So. . . umm. . . if there's a busted link, it's John's fault! Seriously, this has been an easy collaboration between two people who are, in many ways, complete opposites of each other. More on this later.

By this point, you may be asking yourself, *What in the world does any of this have to do with establishing trust?* Well, as you delve into my (Jeff) first-person narrative and my entry into the world of paranormal investigating, *our* (Jeff and John) honesty and candor will emerge through my writing. In other words, my honesty and candor is John's honesty and candor. Quite bluntly, we are on the same qualitative page, and being on the same page has made this collaborative effort work smoothly and well.

Another motivating force in the genesis of this project was our desire to produce a nonfiction book that was honest, candid, devoid of drama, and ego-free, yet relaxed and easy to read—something we believe enthusiasts and the paranormal community at large are hungry for. It has been our experience, in the discussions, emails, and blog dialogues we have had with other investigating teams, that the antics of a few para-celebs have done an incredible disservice to this field of inquiry and to the character of the people who actively participate in it. No one can dispute the valuable contributions made by some early television programs, particularly everyone's favorite paranormal plumbers. However, in the hunger and hype that followed in their trail, a strange and often bizarre cast of characters and celebrity wannabes has been more than willing to serve up easily digestible entertainment to equally hungry production companies.

As these programs grew in popularity, and *ghost hunting* became the latest and greatest form of television entertainment, it became clear that producers were calling the shots, and some of the focus on history, investigating, and evidence review took a backseat to drama and on-screen high jinks. Though all these fun and games may make for "good television," those with a more critical eye (and there are many of us) think, *If this is how these people behave on camera during an investigation, how or why should I believe them when they present their evidence?*

You can argue science and scientific principles and methods until the cows come home, but if you are trying to lend legitimacy to a field of inquiry with so many unknowns, doesn't it require a higher degree of integrity and professionalism?

It is from this perspective that we, like so many other investigating teams, draw serious distinctions among "Paranormal Investigators," "Ghost Hunters," thrill-seekers, paranormal enthusiasts, quacks, hacks, and hooligans/criminals (Google "LeBeau Plantation Fire; St. Bernard Parish, LA"). This brings us to the *voice* of the text (and a shift from first-person plural to first-person singular).

When I first came to this curious endeavor, I found myself hungry for many things. Sure, I wanted answers, but I was also hungry to ask questions and to learn. Frankly, I was tired of being expected to suspend my disbelief and place my trust in a bunch of television yahoos, dramatists, or investigators who were pushing an agenda or trying to achieve pop culture TV stardom. I craved something more balanced, disciplined, and mature—something objective with a healthy dash of skepticism, something that appealed to my sense of logic. This book represents my first steps on that journey of discovery.

Here is my first confession: I envisioned my role in this book as being the objective observer, the journalist if you will, relaying to you my experiences and impressions from my very first plunge into the darkness. Though I have tried to hold true to that cause, my perspective has changed, or rather . . . evolved. It is impossible to take part in this field, to hear what you hear, see what you see, and feel what you feel without being affected. To put it bluntly, there is indeed *something* to this phenomenon, and like so many other investigators, I'm still struggling to put my finger on it.

It is from this perspective that we seek to earn your trust. Why is trust so important? Because we will present evidence for your review and consideration that is both baffling and defies explanation, thus making it paranormal. Other than pushing the volume level where necessary, we have not manipulated, doctored, or otherwise altered any of the clips you will see and hear.

Thus, we ask you to trust us.

1

A Writer's Journey: The Beginning

Whether you're reading this book as a thrill-seeker, an aspiring or experienced paranormal investigator, or simply as a paranormal enthusiast, we all share some common characteristics: a love (okay, a morbid curiosity) of dark, creepy places; an abiding interest in the unknown; and a passion to learn more about, and maybe even to experience, paranormal phenomena. For me, the journey from passive enthusiast to full-fledged investigator began with the explosion of paranormal reality TV and my move to a small rural Ohio town.

Not long after moving from Cleveland's eastern suburbs to the farms and nurseries of Madison, Ohio, I learned of a place just a few miles from my home that was steeped in an odd and mysterious past: the Madison Seminary. More than 170 years old, the Seminary seemed more like a fictional setting for a Stephen King novel than a real historical artifact. From serving as a girls' school to a poorhouse to a home for the mentally impaired, then as a halfway house for Ohio's prison system, the building certainly had plenty of mystery mixed into its blood-red bricks and bleached-bone mortar. Oh—and did I mention that, according to locals, the place is haunted?

I'm a bit of a history geek, a natural offshoot of my formal education, former professions (archaeologist, middle-school teacher), and current vocations (writer and education consultant). So with many questions and few answers, I did what comes naturally to archaeologists: I began digging into the seminary's history. Scouring the shelves of the local and regional libraries and historical societies revealed only a few clues: a document outlining the chain of ownership (paraphrased above), a couple of historical (circa 1910) articles about fund-raising events, and a 1990s article when the building went on the auction block.

Having exhausted my local research avenues, I realized that the real meat I was looking for—the human stories of the residents, occupants, and inmates of the seminary—was in all likelihood locked away within the seminary itself or in some obscure official records facility, far beyond my limited reach. Learning the true stories that took place within the confines of the seminary would require a much more focused and committed effort. Unfortunately for me, the summer was fading and a new school year fast approaching. Researching the Madison Seminary was an activity that would have to wait, at least for the time being.

Of course, putting things on hold only piqued my curiosity. The ghost-hunting programs I watched on TV and their (now para-celebrity) hosts were beginning to investigate equally historic, equally enticing locations, such as boarded-up prisons, hospitals and asylums, forts, and even battlefields. This made the Madison Seminary all the more irresistible. Somehow, some way, I had to get inside and do some paranormal investigating of my own.

Since my research efforts were stymied, I shifted my focus, turning my attention from the traditional avenues of research to the paranormal aspect of the seminary. I learned that the facility had developed a reputation as a hotbed of paranormal activity, making it popular among ghost hunters. I also discovered that the facility was available for overnight investigations for a few hundred dollars and a minimum number of participants. If I truly wanted to get inside, I would need to scrape together the cash and rustle up a group of friends, associates, or like-minded enthusiasts willing to commit to a paranormal adventure.

It felt like I'd hit another brick wall at that point. After all, how does one assemble people for a ghost hunt? I need not tell you that ghost hunting and paranormal investigating used to be a rather dubious endeavor and still raises a lot of eyebrows among the general public. Truth be told, I wasn't ready to admit to anything more than passive enthusiasm.

So what do you do—put an ad in the paper or post a message on Craigslist? **WANTED: Ghost-hunting enthusiasts to conduct paranormal investigation of haunted building!** *That* seemed like a recipe for disaster. Sure, I'd probably find some reasonably responsible adults, but I'd also have to sift through dozens, if not hundreds, of yahoos to find that handful of serious, like-minded people. Then I thought: *Why reinvent the wheel?* Surely there must be established paranormal groups already interested in investigating the seminary.

A strategy quickly emerged. Using a two-pronged approach, I first dug into the seminary's Internet footprint and Facebook page where I found their calendar and a list of the paranormal groups scheduled to conduct investigations at the property. At this point I realized that the seminary had, in fact, developed a positive national reputation in the paranormal investigating community. Teams of paranormal investigators literally traveled hundreds of miles to investigate—burning the gas and paying the cash to come to my little town. Very cool!

Of the teams scheduled, only a few were based in Ohio. I contacted all three, explaining my interest and dilemma. Wanting to immediately put to rest any initial concerns they might have about my seriousness, I explained that I was a local teacher, a history buff, etc., interested in observing them conduct their investigation and helping out as best I could where and when they needed me. I further explained that as a paranormal enthusiast without any group affiliations, getting into the seminary, even here in my own backyard, was virtually impossible. Naturally, I would pay my share of the admission fee and carry my weight (their equipment) as needed.

Of the three teams I contacted, all responded in a week or less. All were sympathetic and highly professional. Two explained that they had a full roster of investigators planning on participating, but they would keep me in mind if there were any cancellations. The founder of the third team, a group based out of central Ohio and scheduled to investigate the building in about eight weeks, explained that he would be open to having an outside observer or participant come along. However, he would first need to consult with his team members before extending an invitation.

Now I was getting somewhere.

The second part of my approach to finding a team was a basic Google search of local paranormal groups. Though there were about a dozen teams in my tri-county area, all of which I reached out to, I received only one reply. Bob, the founder of the group that replied, said he was currently looking to add new members to his team, and if I'd fill out an application on the team's website, he would follow up quickly and let me know if there was a possible spot for me. Cool!

Things were falling into place. Rather than putting all my eggs into one basket, I had successfully established contact and started a meaningful dialogue with two groups: one that was already scheduled to investigate the seminary and the other . . . well, I wasn't sure what their schedule was. So I filled out the online application, where again I explained my personal interests in the paranormal, provided my background details, and readily admitted to lacking any practical experience in paranormal investigating. I did this to convey my honesty, candor, and sincerity.

I think there are important lessons here for both enthusiasts and investigative teams: (1) following through on even basic research produces results; and (2) communication is fundamental to establishing and maintaining a positive image. Following through on my research got me connected with two groups, and those that didn't return my inquiries left a lasting negative impression of their professionalism.

Not long after completing the application, I heard back from Bob, who invited me on his group's next case—an investigation of a municipal cemetery. He explained that one of the city managers had asked him and his group to investigate claims from nearby residents about strange sounds and sightings at the graveyard. According to Bob, neighbors had seen things, including apparitions and shadowy figures, and often reported shrieks and screams coming from the cemetery at all hours of the night. According to his contact, when police responded to the complaints, nothing was ever found.

"Sure," I answered enthusiastically. "Sign me up!"

Shortly after receiving Bob's invitation to apply, I heard from John, the founder of C–Bus Paranormal, the group scheduled to investigate Madison Seminary. Much to my delight, he too invited me to come along on their investigation. I felt like a kid a week before Christmas! Not only had I scored admission into the seminary, I'd found a local group that was beefing up its membership and actively investigating locations in my area. This result was far better than I had expected. I was totally psyched.

My excitement quickly grew as time slowly passed. I bought a cheapo fifteen dollars digital voice recorder to document these adventures and continued working on my other writing projects. As the date for the cemetery investigation neared, my trepidation also rose. Like most people, I'd been to cemeteries before and had even taken part in the funerals of dearly departed friends and family members. Of course, that was all very different; traditionally, we go to cemeteries to bury the dead and to pay our respects, not to attempt to interact with their spirits and document that interaction. The potential goings-on at a cemetery after the grounds are closed, employees leave, and the gates are locked was fodder for the imagination.

I must confess that as the investigation neared, my imagination toyed with me. All paranormal enthusiasts are familiar with the stories, claims, and—to some extent—the evidence shown on TV of shadowy figures and dark masses that move about their haunts. In my mind, however, a cemetery seemed different, particularly at night. Most of the haunted locations popular among investigators are homes or buildings. Cemeteries, solemn repositories of the deceased, struck me as being in a completely different league . . . at least from a paranormal perspective. If there really was something to this paranormal stuff, wouldn't or shouldn't the final resting place of hundreds or even thousands of people be a natural (or even *super*natural) nexus for paranormal phenomena? This intrigue, coupled with Bob's reporting, which I assumed was accurate, set the stage for what I was certain would be a remarkable experience.

Mentor Municipal Cemetery

The date for the cemetery investigation arrived at last. Bob had provided specific instructions on when to arrive and where to park. Ironically, pulling into a cemetery after hours had its own peculiar feel. After all, I was running on faith and nerve; I had never met Bob. Though we'd talked on the phone a couple of times before the investigation, I still had no idea who this guy was or if he and his group were legit. As I drove to the location, I kept wondering, *What if I'm the only schmuck to show up? What if I'm being punked?* What if the cops follow me in and pull me out of my car and start asking reasonable questions like "What the hell are you doing here at this hour of the night? Can't you read the sign; the cemetery is closed!" What if . . . what if?

Thankfully, I was the *second* person to arrive. Now if I got busted, at least I wouldn't be going to the slammer alone. About fifteen minutes later, Bob himself arrived, and over the following thirty minutes, an assortment of twelve other people with flashlights, digital cameras, and voice recorders had gathered at the cemetery's maintenance house.

Bob was a likeable guy and quickly put our minds at rest by explaining that his relationship with the city was ironclad, producing a document (on city letterhead) that acted as a permit, authorizing the investigation. He passed out copies of the document to team leaders in case law enforcement showed up while the groups were separated. This did a lot to calm my nerves, at least about the legal ramifications of being in a municipal cemetery after hours. I have since learned that trespassing on public and private lands for the purpose of ghost hunting is more common than people might think. Though I was indeed very curious about this kind of phenomena, I certainly wasn't keen on spending a night in jail to satisfy that curiosity. At least with Bob's document, I could concentrate without distraction on the real focus of the investigation: to observe, experience, and hopefully capture evidence of paranormal activity.

It was a beautiful late summer night: clear skies, bright moon, warm temperatures, and low humidity—giving the cemetery a serenity I didn't expect. This was neither the macabre landscape my imagination seemed to want nor the cold, austere field of granite markers and tablets I'd expected. Instead, I found myself in a peaceful nocturnal environment. Well-thought-out and maintained, it was organized like a small city with a series of paved parallel roads intersected by wide gravel paths. In the 40-foot x 300-foot rectangular spaces between the paths and pavement lay the neatly manicured gravesites of the interred.

Unlike the Jewish cemeteries I was accustomed to, where wreaths and mementos are not permitted, this cemetery allowed loved ones to place arrangements, artifacts, and vigil lights—small wax candles or solar-powered lights—beside the headstones. Unfamiliar with this custom, I found the vigils really nice, comforting reminders of a lost loved one.

It was finally time to begin the investigation. We broke up into small groups with an experienced team leader in each group. I was fortunate to be partnered with Danielle, who had investigated the cemetery with Bob's group once before. Along with two other newbies, we set off down one of the roads into the cemetery. Moving away from the blazing mercury-vapor-lighted maintenance house, our eyes quickly adjusted to the silvery moonlight and ambient quiet of the summer night.

As we walked down the road toward the farther reaches of the cemetery, Danielle told us about her first experience investigating the cemetery—of hearing whispered voices, disembodied moans and screams, and shadows that seemed to dart out from behind gravestones. As a single mother to a child with serious medical issues, she mentioned her affinity to the children who were buried there. She was, in fact, leading us to the gravesite of one child: little Lisa, who had died at the age of six in the early 1980s. During the previous investigation, Danielle heard a child's laugh at Lisa's gravesite, and she wanted to pay a quick visit to see if her spirit was still around.

The experience had clearly made a profound impression on Danielle. Like a family member expertly weaving around the markers, she knew exactly where she was going and brought our small group to Lisa's final resting place—where a delicate porcelain angel held a twinkling LED light. After placing a small silk flower beside the headstone, Danielle attempted to engage the spirit of Lisa, warmly greeting her and reminding her of their last visit. Danielle introduced us as friends and began a short EVP (Electronic Voice Phenomenon) session, gently encouraging the little girl to laugh or say hello or tell us anything she wanted to. We heard nothing, and upon review of the audio, I detected nothing.

Over the next four hours, I toured the grounds with Danielle and several other group members. Quickly overcoming the creep factor of being in the moonlit cemetery and gaining confidence, I even managed a couple of solo excursions, stopping in secluded areas and running my own EVP sessions. Overall, it was a neat, unique experience. Though there were a couple of times when we heard strange scream-like sounds, it was impossible to say whether the noises were paranormal. Since we were situated in the middle of a suburban neighborhood, the sounds could easily be attributed to cats, possums, or any of an entire cadre of natural causes.

Though the walk was a strange and memorable experience, my initial impressions were of disappointment. For all the hype and anticipation I fed into my own excitement, I found nothing of the experience to be out of the ordinary . . . besides being in a graveyard in the wee hours of the morning. There was nothing that my logical mind perceived as extraordinary and certainly nothing I would deem paranormal.

That is, until I reviewed my audio.

Between all the coffee and excitement, getting to sleep that morning was no easy feat. In retrospect, I didn't appreciate how much physical and emotional energy these adventures can take out of you. Your senses are cranked to hear every little noise, feel every sensation. Then, of course, there was the walking: an "easy" five to eight miles of weaving, strolling, and wandering . . . constantly looking over your shoulder because you feel like you're being followed, or taking a second look because you think you saw a shadow. It's quite draining, which is why I waited a couple of days before returning to the audio recordings I made that night. I wanted to be fully awake, refreshed, and running on all cylinders.

First, let me say that contrary to what you might think or what you may have seen on television, audio review is not as simple and easy as it may seem. It takes time for your mind and hearing to adjust, then focus, on the soft subtleties of the most common EVPs (classified as Class B or C; more on these classifications later), which tend to be soft, almost imperceptible whisperings. Class A EVPs, though less common, are the nuggets of gold that keep investigators investigating.

Once adjusted to the audio playback and the natural sounds that my recorder had picked up (wind, the rustle of leaves in the trees, footsteps, even the creaking of my sneakers), I began noticing brief moments, audio fragments of weirdness— strange, inexplicable sounds like breaths and sighs. Then came the strangest thing I'd ever heard in my life: a freaky feminine moan. It was the weirdest, most exhilarating sound I had ever NOT heard.

bit.ly/ghostlyencounters-mentor

I shouted, "What the hell was that?" when I heard it.

My mind raced back to the hunt and the exact location of the audio capture, which I remembered distinctly. I was with another guy at that spot and remarked about a name on a marker that, at first look, appeared to be the same as my own. As you can hear on the audio, I mention the similarity in name; then there's a bizarre human moan, clear as day and clearly female. I couldn't believe it; I'd caught my first EVP! Though the recorded sound lasts barely a second, its impact was profound. The paranormal bug had bitten me. The weird moan would be the first of ten solid EVPs I caught that night. What a rush!

Here are the best of the cemetery EVPs from my first foray into the paranormal.

bit.ly/ghostlyencounters-mentor

Poring over the audio evidence from the cemetery was really an eye-opening experience. The more I listened and focused, the more I seemed to hear—or thought I could hear—things that were not audible the night of the hunt. In time I came to learn of the phenomenon known as pareidolia: *the imagined perception of a pattern or meaning where it does not actually exist, as in considering the moon to have human features.* They can also occur in an auditory context.

Think of pareidolia as the images of Jesus that have been seen on everything from potato chips to screen doors. Our minds can often lead us to believe that we are seeing or hearing something that's really not there. Though a skeptic might punch holes in some of the more marginal EVPs you have just listened to, the better EVPs, like the freaky moan, are far less ambiguous. Mysterious? Absolutely. Ambiguous? I don't think so.

The Madison Seminary

At long last, my second scheduled adventure, the visit at the Madison Seminary, finally arrived. I was totally psyched. Arriving at the building about thirty minutes early to scope things out, I found that John and Andrew from C-Bus Paranormal (Columbus, Ohio) had arrived even earlier, also to check things out and to get pictures for their website. They greeted me warmly and made me feel welcome. In hindsight, I find it strangely ironic that things went as well as they did. Here I was, the old-guy teacher who would soon be taking directions from these much younger, long-haired metal-heads, men half my age. I later learned that John was the former lead guitarist for a Columbus-area death-metal band. I still laugh when I think about it—not at the idea that I'm a fuddy-duddy or that John and crew are a bunch of rock 'n' roll head bangers. It's just that as I've come to learn, the paranormal, like politics, makes for some strange bedfellows.

As we waited for the owner to arrive and unlock the building, we talked about John's and Andrew's investigating experiences and the paranormal television scene. Though I wanted to be more reporter-like, I'm sure I sounded more like a kid on a sugar rush. I had *so* many questions about John's experiences and the stuff I had seen on television. As John patiently and honestly answered my questions, my respect for him grew. I was listening to a rational, levelheaded fellow. Much like me, he was skeptical of the paranormal programs, the celebs who presented them, and some of the evidence they presented. John, however, was not a skeptic.

Courtesy of Robert Bazzle and Greater Ohio Spirit Trackers.

Courtesy of Madison Historical Society.

What's the difference? In my opinion it is open-mindedness, particularly as it relates to the paranormal. No amount of evidence can prove to a skeptic that a paranormal phenomenon is taking place. On the other hand, being skeptical means dispassionately looking for logical explanations (whether natural or man-made) for extraordinary events or occurrences. When the mystery remains despite your best efforts at disqualifying or explaining a given phenomenon, an open mind can acknowledge that something beyond the ordinary, beyond normal—even something *paranormal*—may be at work. This was John's approach, and all my instincts, academic knowledge, and training told me that this was how it should be done. I was in good hands.

At 9:00 p.m., Tom Cassell (the building owner's grown son) arrived to unlock and admit us to the premises, leading us first into the basement—the facility's former kitchen and employee lunchroom—where fees were paid and liability waivers signed. If I were to trip, fall, and break my neck, it would be all on me.

It's worth noting, especially to passive enthusiasts and readers interested in getting into the investigating scene, that the signed waivers required for access to many of these locations should be taken seriously. Though it's true that the folks who own or operate these locations need to legally cover their butts, usually there are often legitimate structural or environmental reasons why you must sign a waiver. Since the start of my paranormal adventure, I've seen and explored a wide range of locations, from occupied single-family homes, commercial storefronts, industrial warehouses and manufacturing facilities, to dilapidated and crumbling structures, some of which should have been condemned to the wrecking ball.

At some locations, asbestos can fall like snow, black mold can streak the walls, and stairs or entire sections of flooring can be completely collapsed. In many cases, the owners and managers of these structures are rehabilitating, renovating, and (in a few cases) doing complete rebuilds. Monies generated from ghost hunting often provide the funding needed to save many of these historic sites. Obviously, property owners don't want people getting sick or hurt, and usually identify, cordon off, and sometimes completely board off dangerous areas. Though efforts are made to minimize risks, there are no perfect fixes or solutions, which is why you have to be aware, alert, and sign a release. It's okay to take a casual, lighthearted approach to ghost hunting and paranormal investigating. However, you would be foolish to dismiss the potential physical hazards present in some of these places.

Having dispensed with the administrative necessities, Tom began his forty-five-minute tour of the sprawling facility, covering nearly one hundred rooms, four floors, and two buildings. Though the place looks huge from the outside, once inside the size and scope seemed to double. It is truly immense. Leading us through the buildings, he pointed out the various hot spots of activities and descriptions of claims made by other teams of investigators. As a medical professional, Tom's narrative and anecdotes were extremely credible. Like John, he seemed dubious of the more dramatic claims made by some paranormal teams, yet needed no convincing that strange events take place at the seminary.

> At first, I didn't think very much about this paranormal ghost-hunting stuff. This building has been in my family for many years and to me, it was just a big old dusty building. Only when I got older and started spending more time here did I realize that some really strange things go on here. For me, the scariest experience I've had is probably one of the first experiences.

> I was here doing cleanup with a couple of friends on the first floor when we heard a loud racket from one of the back rooms. I thought someone had broken in, so I sent my friends out the front to race around the back, hoping to trap the intruder. When I turned the corner down the corridor where the noises came from I saw a man-sized shadow cross the hallway, leaving one room on one side of the hall to another room on the opposite side of the hall. It scared the crap out of me.

> I ran down the hall and into the room, where I fully expected to find someone. No one was there; none of the windows had been opened; none of the doors closed. I opened the locked window and found my friends checking the back of the building and asked if they saw anyone. Of course they replied "no." I must have looked like a ghost myself, because they started asking me what I saw. I told them I saw a guy, about six feet tall that ran into the room I was standing in.

They suddenly looked like ghosts as they explained, "We didn't see a thing," and "there's nobody out here."

Since that first experience, I have stayed much more alert to the things I've seen and heard in here—the shadows, the voices, the whispering. It's all really wild.

Tom Cassell, Madison Seminary

When Tom wrapped up the tour, John and Andrew jumped into action with me in tow. Four large totes were quickly unloaded from John's car, and the setup officially began. Having done some video production back in my college days, I was generally familiar with what John was doing. What I didn't know was how he'd actually pull it off. After all, this place was big, really big, and there were only three of us.

In short order, C-Bus's technical capabilities—the literal nuts-and-bolts of paranormal investigating—were fully revealed. Their equipment included: a sophisticated DVR (digital video recording) console, a 20-inch monitor, eight static infrared cameras, a dozen reels of cables and cords, two Sony night-vision camcorders, four infrared illuminators, ten audio recorders, a parabolic microphone with headphones, a K2 meter, a Mel-meter, a spirit box (with remote speakers), four geophones (motion detectors with alarms), a laser grid, and bags of backup batteries. This was the real deal and very cool—just like on the paranormal TV shows. Clearly, running a heavy metal band and production company had its advantages.

Not wanting to be in anyone's way, I stepped back and watched as John formulated his plan and set up his equipment. Handing me a reel of video cable, he instructed me to take the line to the top floor, reel out approximately 25 feet of slack cable, then secure it and feed the remaining line down the three flights of stairs and into the kitchen, where he was setting up the makeshift command center. With flashlight in hand, away I went, leaving the lighted kitchen area and John and Andrew to their work.

As I vaulted up the stairs and the darkness closed in on my little beam of light, I suddenly realized I was on my own . . . alone . . . in the dark . . . in a haunted seminary. Whoa!

I'd be lying if I said I wasn't a little scared . . . okay, a *lot* scared. In the weeks preceding the investigation, I had seen YouTube videos chock-full of evidence confirming the seminary's reputation as one of Ohio's most haunted locations. I had also captured my own astounding audio evidence at the cemetery. Now, at last, here I was . . . standing in a dark stairwell, about to enter an even darker floor. The closest sensation I can liken it to is an odd mix of anxiety, exhilaration, and fear. Though we all have knowledge and experience with anxiety and exhilaration, and have developed coping mechanisms to deal with these feelings, fear is a cat of a different breed.

I don't want to give you the wrong impression; I wasn't about to soil myself or turn tail and run out the front door, *as though I'd seen a ghost,* which of course is why I was there in the first place. Fear, at least in this context, is that all-too-clichéd concept of the unknown. Sure, we're all fearful of the unknown and the unfamiliar; however, *this* unknown—this phenomenon I was looking to experience and was now getting my first taste of—is, was, and continues to be very much unknown . . . a true enigma.

I'm sometimes accused of (and sometimes admit to) overthinking things, but as a writer, lifelong student, liberal artist, etc., I couldn't shake the fact that the deeper darkness I was about to enter might challenge every bit of logic and conventional thinking I had acquired in all my years of life. For me, the implications were both profound and a little disturbing.

Rather than dipping in a toe and then slowly creeping into the cold water, I decided, *Screw it, I'm going in* . . . and plunged into the darkness. Yes, I was scared, but now I had a job to do, a simple task to perform. I held the end of my flashlight between my teeth and quickly began pulling cable from the reel. I didn't look right; I didn't look left, I simply unreeled cable. *If I don't look at it, it won't look at me; if I pretend it's not there, it will ignore me . . .* A child's logic was steering the thoughts of a grown man, who was attempting, albeit poorly, to overcome a fear of the dark. Correction: a fear of the dark in a creepy old building . . . double correction: a fear of what was *in* the dark in a creepy old *haunted* building.

Then I felt stupid and collected my wits and courage. In all I had read, listened to, and learned about this place, I had never heard of anyone being hurt . . . at least, not significantly. . . .

With the immediate task completed and a loose pile of cable at my feet, I scanned the large open space of the top floor with my trusty flashlight; no zombies, vampires, white-sheeted bogeymen here, no apparitions or shadows, nothing. *Enough dithering,* I thought. *Time to get your butt in gear; you don't want C-Bus to think you're a slacker.*

In about an hour, we were ready to go: stationary infrared (IR) cameras were set and wired, and digital voice recorders were placed strategically throughout the building. It was time to learn about this building and its mysteries on its own terms. With portable night-vision camcorders, infrared lighting attachments, and audio recorders, we set off as a team into the seminary.

By now the sun had completely set, and the seminary was pitch-black, save for the flickering and splashing white light from our flashlights. Once secure and adjusted to the dark, we turned off the flashlights, relying on the light cast by the camcorder's 2½-inch pop-out screen. Slowly we made our way into the depths of the building, going room to room, floor to floor, taking lots of time to simply listen to the building and conduct several EVP sessions.

It's during these early stages of an investigation, as your senses adjust and sharpen, that you begin getting what I can only describe as a "vibe" for the location—that inexplicable gut sensation that permeates your whole being, a blend of physical, emotional, instinctual, even spiritual stimuli brought on by the ambient environment. The *vibe* is that innate gauge or meter that tells you when the space you occupy is perfectly normal and ordinary—or not. The classic metaphor is when you walk in on an argument and the tension is so thick you can cut it with a knife. Though it's hard to quantify, the seminary had such a vibe—a heavy, uncomfortable feeling like being in a room packed with people and not knowing a single soul.

We began hearing things—subtle sounds of movement in adjacent rooms and other floors. Distant knocks, steps, and clatters. Some sounds were the natural settling of a 170-year-old building, others . . . not so much. Then came the hums and whispers: totally fantastic, totally freaky.

We continued our exploration, higher and deeper into the darkness, eventually finding our way to the fourth floor, where I had nervously laid out the cable. Though a large section of this floor is similar to an open ballroom, a long corridor along the eastern wall leads to a series of smaller rooms, where, according to Tom, the spirits of a belligerent nurse and patient are believed to reside. Tom had warned us about setting equipment near or otherwise blocking a particular doorway in this corridor, noting that it might agitate one of the spirits who was known to knock over cameras or physically lash out at the living. To John and Andrew, this was like an open invitation to block, obstruct, or otherwise interfere with the entity's movement—in other words, to mildly provoke whatever spirit or spirits might be there. While I was on my guard, John and Andrew were looking to stir things up.

John led the way into the hallway. As we neared the small room Tom had cautioned us about, Andrew broke ranks, setting a small chair we had passed directly into the doorway and sitting down in it. After a few moments, Andrew got back up and rejoined us. In the clip that follows, taken from the mobile camcorder John was carrying, you will see the start of a paranormal altercation that still amazes me.

What happened next was truly the strangest thing that I have ever "not" witnessed. Andrew screamed and slammed hard to the floor, face-planting an inch from my heels. It scared the crap out of me.

bit.ly/ghostlyencounters-madison

"What the f—," I shouted, nearly jumping out of my skin.

Suddenly realizing we literally had a man down, my paternal instincts jumped into gear and I was instantly hovering over Andrew, checking him out for what had to be a horrific injury. Writhing on the floor, Andrew was clearly in severe pain.

"Something pushed me, HARD!" he moaned.

John was pissed. "Son of a bitch! We didn't give you permission to touch us!"

With cameras and voice recorders still rolling, we sat Andrew up and checked him out more thoroughly. Despite having had the wind knocked out of him from the fall, there were no apparent serious injuries.

This seemed like a good time to take a break. As I helped Andrew down the hallway toward the staircase, John fumed, "I'll be back—I guarantee it. You want to get physical with someone, you come after me. I dare you."

Obviously, we were all pretty riled up: Andrew getting decked, John fired up about one of his crew getting assaulted . . . and me in the middle, completely baffled by what had just happened. I truly didn't know what to make of the episode.

I have to admit that my first thoughts were that Andrew had slipped or tripped. However, when we reviewed the audio and video we collected, my paranormal world was rocked.

bit.ly/ghostlyencounters-madison

Though Andrew's fourth-floor altercation (and the associated EVP) was the most dramatic event of the night, the audio evidence underscored Madison Seminary's reputation as one of Ohio's most active paranormal sites. With more than a dozen EVPs found on voice recorders and the audio portion of the video apparatus, Madison remains a highlight of my overall paranormal experience and a favored location to investigate. Here are my handpicked favorites from that first experience in the Madison Seminary.

bit.ly/ghostlyencounters-madison

There's no doubt: after reviewing my own audio and listening to the higher quality evidence from the C-Bus equipment, the proverbial hook had been set. Like an addict, I wanted more . . . I needed more.

2

Technical Stuff: Keeping It Real, Keeping It Basic

Audio Basics

Whether you are an inexperienced enthusiast looking to take your first steps into the darkness, a ghost-hunting thrill-seeker, or looking to become a full-fledged paranormal investigator, dependable audio and/or video equipment is essential for documenting your adventures. Remember, without recorded audio or video, your greatest paranormal experience will be nothing more than a personal memory, fodder for late nights around the campfire.

Contrary to what you might think, decent start-up equipment need not break the bank. Depending on your overall objectives, you can spend as little as $25 for basic audio and around $200 for a night-vision camcorder, perhaps less if you find something used. Of course for the techno-geeks, the sky is truly the limit in terms of quality equipment and accessories. But for the purposes of our discussion, we will limit our review to the basic essentials—key pieces of data-collecting technology and accessories that range from entry to mid-level price points: keeping it real, keeping it basic. These devices represent the core of C-Bus Paranormal's inventory.

In the realm of paranormal evidence, there are two types of vocal evidence: the disembodied voice and the EVP. A disembodied voice, as the name implies, is a physically audible human voice that seems to come from nowhere, no one, nobody. An EVP (electronic voice phenomenon), also as the name implies, is a voice that is captured on an electronic device, typically a digital voice recorder or camcorder.

EVPs are generally classified as either a Class A, Class B, or Class C EVP.

- **Class A** - This type of EVP is loud, clear, and of very high quality. The voice is easily understandable and does not need enhancement or amplification. Class A EVPs are also often (but not always) in direct response to a question being asked.
- **Class B** - This is the most common type of EVP. This type of EVP is of a somewhat lower quality and clarity than a Class A EVP but still very audible. Class B EVPs often do need some degree of enhancement or amplification to be heard clearer. The voice may not be clear enough to be totally understood, or there may be disagreement as to what it is saying. Class B EVPs are often not in direct response to a question.
- **Class C** - This is the lowest quality EVP. With a Class C EVP even the best enhancement and amplification may not be sufficient to make the voice audible or clear. There may even be debate whether or not an EVP is actually present.

Definitions by Michael Cardinuto and Long Island Paranormal Investigators.

Since the majority of captured evidence is audio, your first piece of equipment should be a decent digital audio recorder. How do we define "decent"? A decent recorder is one that provides good quality recording and minimal background (white) noise on playback, minimum 1 GB built-in memory with an easy to operate internal filing system.

Perhaps the most popular audio recorder on the investigating scene also happens to be one of the cheapest: the RCA VR5320. At a cost of approximately twenty-five dollars, the VR5320 provides everything you need in a two-AAA battery device. With 1 GB built-in memory (approximately two hundred hours of recording time), a super convenient slide-out USB plug, and the RCA Digital Voice Manager System (internal filing system with WAV file converter), you couldn't ask for a better package for the price.

RCA VR5320

Though cost-effective and convenient, the unit has its drawbacks. Its initial setup is not very intuitive and working through its functions is somewhat tedious. Though the manual gets you through it all, the unit takes some getting used to, requiring both practice and patience. Perhaps its biggest drawback is its inability to do quick rewinds and playbacks. Perhaps you have just recorded something and you are uncertain if it was a voice or a draft in the chimney. This recorder does not have the capability to stop, rewind, and play back what you recorded moments ago. To play back what you just recorded requires starting the playback at a designated "book mark" or the beginning of the file, which can be a real pain in the butt, especially if you are an hour into an audio session.

In spite of its drawbacks, the RCA VR5320 is a great device. The C-Bus team owns eight of these units for use as both handheld recorders and stationary devices. Simply set it down at a designated location, let it run all night, and pick it up at the end of the investigation. Despite its drawbacks, for twenty-five dollars you can't go wrong.

For approximately thirty-five dollars more, we step up from the RCA to the Olympus WS-801 digital voice recorder. This dandy little unit provides the same functionality as the RCA, with improved sound quality on replay, twice the memory (2 GB/500 hours recording time), and the instant rewind/playback feature . . . for those who just can't wait to get home and download your audio files.

Olympus WS-801

From the RCA and Olympus recorders, we take a quantum leap up to the Zoom H1 digital recorder. With all the internal functions of the RCA and Olympus recorders, the H1 provides superior recording quality, far surpassing the range and richness of cheaper units. Originally designed for the music industry, the H1 has been well received by the paranormal investigating community for its outstanding recording clarity. Commonly referred to as *live audio*, the H1 and similar higher-end units allow investigators to listen and record simultaneously, a feature not found on either the RCA or Olympus.

Though the H1 lacks a built-in USB port, requiring a patch cord to hook up to your PC or laptop, its outstanding sound quality more than makes up for what otherwise is a minor inconvenience. Retailing online at approximately one hundred dollars, the H1 really does provide superior audio recording technology that makes aficionados sit up and take notice. Hear for yourself the difference between these audio clips—one recorded by the RCA, the other by the Zoom H1. You be the judge.

ZOOM H1 Digital Recorder

bit.ly/ghostlyencounters-audio

Video Basics

Generally speaking, 99 percent of the evidence obtained during an investigation is audio based, leaving a scant 1 percent in the realm of video. Legitimate video evidence of paranormal phenomena represents the rarest form of evidence captured. Whether you've caught a slamming door, a black mass, or a full-blown apparition, quality night-vision video apparatus is essential to documenting these rarest of jewels.

Unlike the digital voice recorders, there is no getting off cheap when it comes to decent video equipment and technology. For video, you get what you pay for and if you decide to get night-vision video on the cheap, you will in all likelihood come to regret it. As a former death-metal guitar god, John has always been partial to the Sony product line, both audio and video. That is why C–Bus Paranormal owns two Sony SR45 night-vision camcorders.

These lightweight dandies are easy to operate and provide exceptional video and audio quality in virtually any environment. And yes, the quality of audio should be a consideration when choosing a camcorder. With 40X optical zoom, 2000X digital zoom, 30 GB internal hard drive, 5.1 channel (audio) recording, 2.7-inch touch-screen display, and of

Sony SR45

course the Sony name, you'd be hard-pressed to find a handycam of better quality with more functionality for three hundred dollars (Amazon.com).

In addition to the Sony SR45s, C-Bus Paranormal also employs an eight-channel Zmodo IR DVR (digital video recording) system. Originally designed for the security and surveillance industries, night-vision DVRs have made a profound impact on the field of paranormal investigating. Using wide-angle, stationary IR cameras, DVR systems enable investigators to effectively observe and record large areas and spaces over the course of the entire investigation. Though DVR systems are not without their own limitations, such as the need for electricity (not all locations have readily accessible power), lots of cable to hard wire each camera to the console, and somewhat limited camera range, DVRs still provide invaluable support to serious investigating.

Zmodo 8-Channel DVR (Digital Video Recorder)

Base to mid-range DVR systems are generally four- or eight-channel systems, meaning you can attach up to four or up to eight individual cameras to the system. An 8CH system, like the one pictured above, with cameras, will generally run approximately $300 (Amazon.com). Of course that does not include the cost of cables or a monitor.

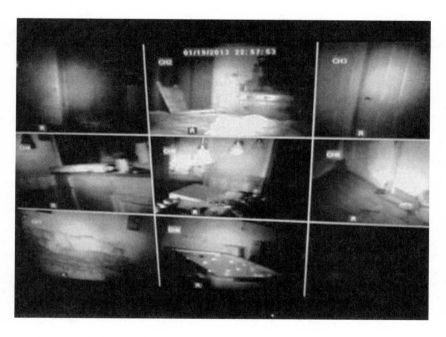

Monitor view of the DVR system fully deployed; at the Painesville residence investigation.

Important Accessories

As you contemplate whether to stick in a toe or jump right in to the paranormal technology pool, there are a few important accessories that will definitely make your investigating experience more productive and even a little more comfortable. First, the most obvious and most frequently forgotten accessory is the battery. Remember, none of these remote technologies work without batteries. Seems simple? The truth of the matter is that everything you have heard or seen on TV relating to battery drain in paranormal situations is unequivocally true.

There are many reasons why equipment fails and batteries drain in environments where paranormal phenomena occur. It is widely believed that entities will absorb or use accessible energy sources, such as battery power, to manifest themselves visibly or audibly. It is also a fact that ambient temperatures can directly affect the energy stored in a battery or the rate a device utilizes energy. Colder temperatures and humid environments, indoors or out, are notorious battery killers. It is also an inescapable fact that sometimes bad batteries come off the assembly line. That's why no self-respecting investigator leaves the house without an ample supply of backup battery power. For camcorders, both standard and extended-life rechargeable batteries should be readily available. Regardless of which make and model you choose, you would be foolish not to invest in at least two additional batteries that are fully charged before your investigation.

As for voice recorders and digital cameras which commonly use AA or AAA batteries, we keep an ample supply of both in backup. Though rechargeable batteries are fine to start with, they are not immune to the life-sucking effects of the environment, paranormal phenomena, or simply extended use. While we are on the subject of batteries, let's tackle the burning question we are often asked: which battery is best, bronze top or bunny batteries? It may surprise you, but we believe spending big bucks on big name batteries is a big waste. Thank god for the various dollar stores!

To each his own, but for our part, we would much rather pay one dollar for a pair of AAs than four dollars. Though the savings factor may not seem like much, you will quickly learn with each investigation you participate in that these devices just love to eat batteries . . . and eat, they will. In fact, on a typical eight-hour investigation you should plan on replacing voice recorder batteries at least once, possibly even twice, depending on the temperature and environment.

As a final thought on the subject of batteries, you don't want to wait until your device is flashing "low battery" before replacing them. Like your cell phone, once you drop to one bar, you'd better change your battery. *(Note: As a life member of the Murphy Society—whatever can go wrong, will go wrong—know you are going to feel pretty foolish when you're in some freaky insane asylum in the middle of nowhere USA, your recorder dies, and you're out of batteries.)*

For those of you who decide to get into the night-vision video scene, your camcorder will likely need enhanced or additional IR light. Though some night-vision camcorders come equipped with built-in IR lamps, they seldom have the power to effectively light your entire field of view while cutting your camcorder's battery power in half. You will definitely need to invest in an IR illuminator. IR illuminators are small battery-powered attachments that project infrared light. Though barely visible to the naked eye, these little darlings turn pitch-black rooms into well-lit spaces for your night vision equipment.

L: Phantom Lite IR flood lamp. R: Vortex IR illuminator.

This image was taken with the second of our two Sony
SR45 night vision camcorders. What appears as bright white
light is actually infrared lighting from the attached IR
illuminator, only detectable with night vision equipment.
If you were standing in the room when this image was
taken, the only visible light would be reflected glare
from the camcorders' viewfinders and nine faint red
LEDs from each of the attached IR illuminators.

There are many varieties of IR illuminators on the market that can be purchased starting at fifty dollars. The difference between these units and their cost relates to the number of IR LEDs. The more IR LEDs, the more IR light; the more IR light, the more area you illuminate, thus the higher cost. Having worked with both the Phantom and Vortex, we can heartily recommend both.

Though there are other equally effective illuminators on the market, we caution against any illuminator that operates off a built-in rechargeable battery. As previously mentioned, malfunctions and particularly battery drains are common occurrences during investigations. In addition, we have both read countless reviews (technical horror stories) of rechargeable IR lamps that crap out after twenty minutes of use and then require several hours of recharge time. If you don't want to be left literally in the dark, get a unit with replaceable battery power.

For relative ease and comfortable extended use of your video equipment during an investigation, we recommend both a camcorder bracket and monopod. Both accessories are relatively inexpensive and will ultimately save your hands, wrists, and arms from hours in an uncomfortable position.

Though these items may seem unnecessary, the truth is (1) not all night-vision camcorders have mounting shoes (small brackets that hold or connect attachments to the camera), and

(2) holding a camcorder and illuminator at or near eye level quickly advances from tedious to uncomfortable to downright painful. Although the camcorder bracket provides some additional flexibility of handling, it's the expandable monopod that makes the night-vision video setup complete.

Fully collapsed, the monopod allows for comfortable ergonomic camera handling while walking or maneuvering through a location. If stationary for an extended period of time, simply extend the leg and lock it into position, thus resting the weight of your gear on the monopod. When you consider the camcorder bracket is under ten dollars and monopods start at around fifteen dollars (Amazon.com), it's easy to see why these gems can make long nights in a haunted house so much easier and comfortable. *(Note: Now if someone would only come up with collapsible chair I can strap to my butt, I'd be in seventh heaven!)*

3

Getting Smart in the Deepening Dark

"Mentor's Most Haunted"

Something very positive had emerged from the Madison Seminary experience, namely an abiding mutual respect between John and me. I liked the way John conducted his investigation. He was patient, dispassionate, and organized. And I later learned that he liked the way I took direction, asked reasonably intelligent questions, and (like him) was equally skeptical of many of the claims of evidence. John and I were clearly on the same page.

Less than a week after the Madison adventure, Bob and the local team announced another expedition to a location he referred to as "Mentor's Most Haunted." Again, this would be a city-invited investigation—this time at an outdoor nature preserve where strange sights and sounds had supposedly been reported. The city had asked that Bob *not* to refer to the location by its specific name. According to Bob, the city claimed they had enough problems keeping teens and other locals out of the area after dark, and word of a paranormal investigation would only compound the problem. Since everything was so hush-hush, we would meet at Bob's house, then follow him to the location.

I was thrilled to learn that Bob had invited the C-Bus crew to participate and that John had accepted the invitation. Having begun to formulate opinions about both groups, I realized this investigation would give me an opportunity to see how well two completely different teams might—or might not—work together. Bob's group was a loosely organized group of approximately twelve friends and enthusiasts. Though limited to personal voice recorders, cameras, and a few EMF (electromagnetic field) meters and EMF pumps, they seemed equally devoted and passionate in their investigations. Conversely, John and the smaller five-member C-Bus team were more technically advanced, both in diversity and quality of equipment. As previously described, the C-Bus team had full audio and video capability that could easily rival any small private investigating firm, not to mention several of the teams seen on TV.

On the night of the "Mentor's Most Haunted" investigation, the team met up as planned at Bob's home. Once again, John and Andrew were early, so as Bob got his act together, John, Andrew, and I reveled in our exploits at the seminary and the preliminary evidence we had captured. I must confess that, though I was a member of Bob's group, I was far more interested in working with John and Andrew. Besides having better equipment, C-Bus was clearly more focused and intent on capturing quality evidence.

As the number of participants continued to climb, I learned that Bob had also invited another paranormal team to join in: a team from Cleveland, which I will refer to as Big City Paranormal. I found this a little perplexing. Granted, we would be in a relatively large outdoor setting, much larger than the cemetery had been—yet with so many people investigating, I wasn't sure how anyone could maintain any level of order or control. And with so many people trampling through the woods at the same time, each with some kind of recording device, how in the world do you prevent one group of investigators from contaminating the recordings of another? It doesn't take a rocket scientist to see this was not a well-conceived strategy.

John was in total agreement, yet in spite of these concerns, we held our tongues. We were, after all, invited guests—and raising objections or concerns with Bob would be rude. This was his investigation. He was in charge.

Approximately ten cars with twenty-five people followed Bob to the parking area of "Mentor's Most Haunted." By the time we arrived, the weather had soured. Though the cool temperature was no deterrent, a light on-again, off-again drizzle prevented John from breaking out his night-vision camcorders. This would be an audio-only event.

Bob didn't seem to mind that I was hanging with John and Andrew, so there I stayed. We were also joined by Julie, a veteran investigator who, like Bob, lived locally. She too was new to Bob's group but was familiar with the C-Bus team, having met them at a public investigation of Moundsville Penitentiary in West Virginia the previous spring. Frequently accompanied by her husband, Mick, Julie brings a little bag of tricks—an interesting mix of old-school and new technologies. Neatly stored in two medium-sized cosmetics bags, Julie packed a night-vision camcorder with IR attachment, two digital voice recorders, Mel and Trifield (EMF) meters, a spirit box, and dowsing rods. The only thing she seemed to be missing was a DVR system and Ouija board.

When the collection of participants had assembled at the trailhead, Bob provided a description of the activity that supposedly took place throughout the area. Floating lights and disembodied voices were the most frequent reports. Two points of interest to me were a small family burial plot dated from the mid-1800s and a prehistoric Native American habitation site discovered and excavated in the 1980s. There was no question: the area was rich in both history and prehistory.

The family plot is a surviving feature from one of the area's earliest homesteaders, Henry Marshall Brooks (1809–1883). Though Henry is buried at the Mentor Municipal Cemetery, the graves in the nature preserve are those of his first wife and two daughters—children from each of his two marriages. As for the archaeological aspect, excavation reports indicate two significant periods of prehistoric habitation, during the Archaic Period (1600–1000 BC) and the Late Woodland Period (AD 1000–1600). This area was also quite prominent during our nation's frontier years and founding, as well as during the War of 1812, when naval battles on the Great Lakes were frequent. It seemed to me there was a lot of potential for paranormal activity in the area.

Breaking up into our small four- and five-person teams, we entered the nature area, following the paved walking path. As we walked, I asked Bob to describe the historical events that might be linked to the paranormal phenomena taking place. He explained that during early frontier days, Native American tribes supposedly massacred a group of early settlers. Then in the nineteenth century, there was a small homestead on the property, as evidenced by the small family plot we would visit a few times over the course of the evening. Bob went on to explain that much more recently, the authorities had found a deranged drunkard in the area who supposedly claimed responsibility for killing his wife and burying her body at some still-undiscovered location in the preserve.

Though the anecdotes were interesting, I was troubled by Bob's consistent use of the term *supposedly*. I gently pressed the issue, noting his mention of police being called to the location because of mysterious sights and sounds, floating lights, and disembodied voices. "Is there documentation of these stories about the drunken killer . . . complaints filed, police reports?" I asked.

"No," he replied. "The police weren't allowed to file reports on the things they saw. Supposedly (there was that word again!), several of the responding officers suspiciously retired shortly after receiving the call." *What?*

I cleared my throat, struggling to stifle a laugh. "How interesting," I replied casually.

These stories had more holes than a slab of Swiss cheese. Not that I expected handwritten journals or historical documents, but come on, what the hell were we doing here, playing Scooby-Doo and Mystery Inc.? Again I held my tongue. Bob had delivered a paranormal experience at the cemetery, so maybe there was more here than met the eye . . . or ear. Maybe there was a real mystery here, waiting to be discovered, or maybe I was feeling a little snobby and expecting way too much of Bob.

Maybe . . . maybe not. Though I kept quiet, I was not a happy camper. I felt myself changing; I was becoming an investigator, a keen observer of the people and processes involved in investigating. In the short time I had been participating in these investigations, I had seen, heard, and experienced some pretty wild things, all of which were rooted in a specific historical context. Bob's tales of *the supposed*, however, were sticking in my throat. Chasing legends might be fine for some folks, but for me, chasing legends was like chasing a puff of smoke in a windstorm. At the cemetery, I didn't need documentation or context about the departed; I was surrounded by them. Though I would have liked and indeed sought evidence of the people who had resided at the seminary, I was within the building: a tangible, well-documented historical artifact. Now it seemed I was chasing will-o'-the-wisps, while getting rained on and being eaten by the last of the year's marsh flies and mosquitoes.

When we reached the central hub of the walking trail, Bob and several others cut north. John, Andrew, Julie, and I continued east, preferring to get away from the larger collection of people. For four hours, we wandered the trails and woods of "Mentor's Most Haunted," finding the small family plot and conducting numerous EVP sessions, while at the same time trying to figure out what unsuspecting people might see or interpret as paranormal phenomena, floating lights, and disembodied voices.

That night, John got great use out of his parabolic microphone: a handheld radar-dish-like device that does an incredible job of picking up soft and distant noises. Though occasionally startled by the hooting of owls, the chatter of other nocturnal rodents, the glowing eyes of deer, and the distant revelry (lights and sounds) of partiers at a nearby yacht club, we observed nothing extraordinary and certainly nothing paranormal.

Was the investigation of "Mentor's Most Haunted" a waste of time? It depends on how you look at it. For me it was a valuable learning experience. Would I do it again? No way! After doing my own post-investigation research, I discovered all the bodies once buried at the homestead site had been removed and reburied at the Mentor Municipal Cemetery in the 1870s. In a 1998 newspaper article discussing the nature preserve and the homestead burials, a city official chuckled "over the thought that the city might be guarding a burial ground with nobody in it."[1]

Lesson learned: an hour of research can save you hours of investigating.

A Windy Night in Painesville

After the "Mentor's Most Haunted" case, I maintained contact with Julie, who, like the C-Bus team, had strong opinions about how to investigate the paranormal. In turn, she shared with the C-Bus team an invitation from a friend who was interested in having an investigation of her private residence, in Painesville, Ohio. Originally built in the 1860s, the home was in the process of a major rehab which had apparently stirred up some unsettling paranormal activity.

---

[1]   Ott, Thomas; "A Grave Position For Mentor To Be In, It's Not Certain Stone Really Marks Remains," *Cleveland Plain Dealer*, December 8, 1998, Pg 1B

Naturally, investigations in private homes present a slew of challenges you don't typically find in haunted buildings or sites that charge an admission fee—most notably, the fact that such places are still inhabited by the living. These types of investigations require a high degree of sensitivity, respectability, and discretion. You can't simply plant IR cameras in peoples' closets or dressers. Even though you have been invited into a private residence with the hopes of capturing evidence to validate a homeowner's claim, it's wrong to presume that curious eyes and digital recording technologies are going to be welcome in every square inch of a household.

I was very much looking forward to this unique investigation. Obtaining evidence of paranormal phenomena was certainly important, but from an observational perspective I also wanted to see how John worked in a private residence, where the paranormal claims were subjective, meaning the observations were limited to the occupants and frequent visitors.

The night of the investigation took place in early November. A cold northerly wind blowing across Lake Erie seemed to sweep the clouds from the sky, leaving an incredible starry expanse that allowed temperatures to plummet fast. We met up at 8:00 p.m. and were welcomed by Karen and her eldest son, Brian. By now I was comfortable working with John, but was keen to observe how he would handle the interview of the homeowners.

Having a lot of experience conducting interviews from my college days, I was acutely aware of how interviewers can often lead respondents in a particular direction—sometimes knowingly, other times not. Remember, there are no formal classes for paranormal investigating, and if you have no background or experience in conducting an interview, you may be completely biased in your inquiry without even knowing it.

Though the interview was informal, John did an effective job of maintaining his objectivity. He inquired about the history of the house and what the homeowners knew or had learned about their home since its purchase. He made inquiries into the nature of the renovations they were engaged in, specifically about structural changes and electrical updates. Of course, John also queried about the paranormal activity they experienced.

Prior to the investigation, and armed with little more than an address, John and I dug into public records, discovering that the house was originally built in 1862 and was the farmstead for a parcel in excess of four hundred acres. Though the property remained in the family of the original homesteaders for nearly one hundred years, the farm was gradually parceled off to pay for expenses and an ever-increasing tax burden. In the 1960s, descendants of the original owners finally divested themselves of the property and sold the home with its remaining fourteen acres. The current owners, who had been in the home for about ten years, were knee-deep in renovations, having spent their first years and many thousands of dollars stabilizing and waterproofing the foundation and basement. This included the dismantling of an old back porch, which was converted into a mud/laundry room, a renovation which produced some interesting archaeological evidence. Items discovered buried under the old porch included several turn-of-the-century farm implements, a few (intact) pieces of china, and a rather nasty small-animal leg trap.

More recent updates included a complete electrical overhaul and a kitchen rebuild, which uncovered several shoes within the interior walls. Placing shoes in walls is a well-known, well-documented custom of the eighteenth and nineteenth centuries, intended to ward off evil spirits.

Though the historic artifacts were intriguing, the paranormal experiences Karen and Brian claimed to have witnessed were even more enticing. Both had seen what they described as a six-foot-tall shadow figure that moved about the living room, dining room, and kitchen. More frequently, they saw the apparition of a cat darting from the basement door into the kitchen, much to the displeasure of the actual mouser-in-residence. The most common of the unexplained occurrences was the banging of the new kitchen cabinet doors and drawers, activity which occurred during the day and night.

Although the homeowners were frequently startled by these indiscriminate events, they acknowledged that they did not feel threatened, and whoever or whatever was present in the house was not malicious. Their goal in having us investigate was simply to validate their claims and perhaps to capture audio or video evidence of the phenomena. This would certainly be a unique investigation.

With the interview complete and a plan in mind, John directed the setup, sending Julie and me to specific locations in the house to set and wire the static IR cameras. In about forty minutes we were ready to go, with cameras covering all the bedrooms, the kitchen, dining room, and the basement. For the next five hours, John, Julie, the two homeowners, and I actively investigated various rooms throughout the house, with Julie's husband Mick watching the DVR monitors for any activity we couldn't see in the unoccupied rooms. Though we heavily relied on our audio recorders and night-vision camcorders, we also used several other common devices for paranormal investigating, such as motion detectors (a.k.a. geophones) and a spirit box, which is a device that sweeps the AM and FM radio bands, creating a white-noise background that spirits are supposedly able to communicate through. Interestingly enough, when we deployed the spirit box, we got one discernible response, "Jeff."

bit.ly/ghostlyencounters-painesville

Totally unexpected . . . totally freaky!

Unlike the seminary, a place that had a palpable vibe, there was nothing unusual to the feel of this house . . . that is, until approximately 1:00 a.m., when things started to get noisy.

While conducting an EVP session in the kitchen, we began hearing movement in the basement—a sound like that of boxes being shifted. Of course, we changed our focus to the basement, quickly moved downstairs, and attempted to engage and cajole whatever might be there to communicate with us and make its presence known. That's when a hall door on the second floor closed, sending an audible bang throughout the house and everyone inside it. All of us damn near jumped out of our skin.

"I got that," Mick called out from the DVR setup in the dining room. Of course we all raced up the stairs to see what was captured. The video was rewound and reviewed, and sure enough, a second-floor hallway door that was left open had slammed shut, apparently of its own accord.

bit.ly/ghostlyencounters-painesville

After reviewing the video, John and I went up to study the door and see if there was some natural cause or explanation just off-screen or off-camera to explain the incident. We double-checked the door to see if it was out of balance or alignment, something that might make it close on its own. We checked the hinges to see if the pins were secure, over-lubricated, or anything else that might allow the door to easily travel, such as a shift in air flow caused by the opening of another door in the house, perhaps even the furnace kicking on. We found nothing extraordinary or unusual about the door, the framing, or the knob's mechanism.

"What about this attic door?" John asked from the back hallway. "I don't remember this door being open."

Interesting observation . . . To be perfectly honest, I didn't remember noticing the door during our initial walk-through with the owners. Thankfully, everybody else did, and Karen noted that the attic door had in fact been closed—so much for my keen powers of observation. I did, however, realize the back door was now wide open to the cold night air, which I brought to the attention of the group. This, of course, begged the question: who was the last person in or out? Answer: Brian, the homeowners' son, who left to take his girlfriend home and returned shortly before the slamming incident. Let me add that Brian is a grown adult and leaving the door ajar upon his return, particularly on a frigid autumn night, is not typical behavior.

"I swear I closed it!" he protested.

"Oh, I forgot to mention," Karen piped up. "That happens all the time."

Really! We all looked at each other with curious surprise. In my mind, this changed everything. However, in later discussions with John, he revealed that nothing had changed for him. Though certainly curious, he was rock solid in wanting to see all the video feeds and reviewing all the audio before rendering an opinion.

As the discussion continued, we all took note of the stiff wind that was now steadily blowing. Could the attic door have worked its way open, and a later gust created a vacuum that pulled the hallway door shut? Could the ruckus we heard before the door slam actually have been from the attic, not from the basement? Could Brian have inadvertently left the door ajar and after opening, a gust of wind slammed the upstairs door? We were suddenly buried in a slew of new questions that had us trying different ways to get the upstairs door to slam, such as opening and closing the exterior door with the attic door open and then closed. Though our efforts to replicate the door slamming event did in fact get the upstairs door to move, nothing produced a result that came close to the door-closing we caught on video.

Was the event paranormal? After a thorough review of all the audio and video, and considerable debate among the team, we eventually agreed that the phenomena we experienced in Painesville, though enticing, was nonetheless . . . inconclusive. There were too many variables that prevented us from coming to a unanimous conclusion that involved the paranormal. We would need to conduct another investigation sometime in the future. Without additional and corroborating video or audio, it would be inappropriate to label the limited events we experienced as otherworldly.

It's important to point out that our conclusions do not infer that the homeowners' experiences are not valid or legitimate. Our findings were based exclusively on the data we collected and reviewed. For me, the Painesville house was, like all my investigative experiences, an important learning experience, both technically and evidentiary. Since that investigation, we have become even more careful about the placement of our static cameras, doing our best to keep views unobstructed. As for the evidence or lack thereof, I believe it was extremely worthwhile to experience an investigation where the events were marginal. I think it would have been easy for a less experienced team to go in and record the same data and come out with a completely different interpretation.

Does that mean that the house is not haunted? Hardly. I do, however, think it's worth remembering that the very nature of *investigating*, as the term explains, is "to search out and examine the particulars of a phenomenon in an attempt to learn the facts about something hidden, unique, or complex, especially in an attempt to find a motive or cause" (dictionary.com).

In my opinion, this fundamental tenet of investigating applies to the manner in which data is collected, reviewed, and interpreted, and the overall conduct of the investigation from beginning to end. The application of this tenet, or at least my interpretation of it, was tested and fully illustrated in my next and final investigation with Bob and the local group.

Crash and Burn at the Tanning Salon

After the Painesville house, I received an email from Bob inviting me to take part in another joint investigation with Big City Paranormal, the team from Cleveland. This was the same team that had joined in at the "Mentor's Most Haunted" investigation. This time, Big City would be hosting and we would be the guests. Where, and precisely what type of building, would be revealed once we arrived. *Uh oh*, I thought, *another mystery location*. This was not a good sign—and to be candid, I was getting fed up with the unnecessary cloak-and-dagger nature of these investigations. If you can't trust your team to be discreet about the locations you are investigating, what does that say about the team?

The truth is, I was also growing frustrated with Bob's ambivalence to organization, his absence of background knowledge, and lack of preparation for these investigations. So why did I go, especially if I was steamed by his style of investigating? I put up with it because I was still chomping at the bit and jumping, albeit blindly, at any opportunity to experience the paranormal. At the same time, I was also maturing as an investigator, recognizing the practical connections between my former life as a social scientist and experiences, and their relationships to this new area of interest for me.

Perhaps I should beg your pardon for being so critical, but I have been around much science and taught too many classes on the Scientific Method in my life not to recognize bad practices when I see them. Call me a stickler, but to me, intellectual honesty is also about personal integrity. Although I was still very much a newbie at this paranormal investigating thing, I had an inherent understanding of its objectives and strong beliefs about how these excursions should be conducted.

If the goal is to obtain as much uncontaminated audio and video as possible—what I view as raw data—with the hopes of extracting instances of paranormal phenomenon (the evidence), then you simply can't have dozens of people trampling over each other. This was precisely the situation we walked into at—of all places—a storefront tanning salon on the west side of Cleveland. Pardon the pun, but it was a hot mess from the get-go and made everyone present look like idiots.

When we arrived at the small salon, it was pouring rain, and members from both teams invaded the place like a busload of tourists at a rest stop. I felt awful for the owners of the building, who stared wide-eyed as fifteen people filed into their tiny storefront boutique that looked like it could comfortably fit six on a busy day. Though there were actually four floors open to investigate, it was clear the size of the assembly was not what the owners had anticipated. Quickly getting a grip on the situation, they hustled us into the basement, where we shook off the rain, got rid of our coats, and got the low-down on the premises— which wasn't very much.

According to the owners, the building was erected in the 1890s as a clinic, and later converted into an army hospital after the outbreak of World War I. After the war, the building was turned over to a group of doctors who continued its operation as a clinic/ hospital for another twenty-five years. The multistory building was then sold and converted into retail space on the ground floor and offices on the upper floors. Ultimately, the commercial property was once again sold and the upper floors were divided: half for office space, half converted into apartment units. At the time of the investigation, all of the office spaces were vacant.

We were led on a walk through the three floors of office space and instructed to be extremely quiet, so as not to disturb the tenants who occupied the back side of the building. The walk-through concluded where it began: in the basement, where we were shown additional storage spaces and a locked room that was *supposedly* a morgue back when the building operated as a hospital.

Being the curious chap that I am, I had a lot of questions about the place: was it a tuberculosis hospital at any point—or a mental health facility? How many beds and patients was the facility equipped to handle? Were there any specific events that took place at the building, such as fire, epidemic diseases, perhaps even illegal activity—anything that could be traced in the historic record? Unfortunately, the owners didn't have any additional details about the history of the building, which for me was a real bite in the butt. Oh well, enough jibber-jabber, it was time to see if our army of investigators could substantiate the owners' claims of apparitions, dark masses, and disembodied voices.

Sherry, whom I'd met at Mentor Municipal Cemetery, joined me in a quiet fourth-floor office, far away from the main body of other investigators. Using a Mel-meter, we found some EMF spikes near a few electrical outlets and along the ceiling, where I assume an old-style electrical conduit ran, powering all the offices on the floor. No surprises there. As we settled in and began speaking to whatever or whoever might be present and listening, the footsteps of other investigators filtered through the paper-thin walls—not very helpful or encouraging. Within ten minutes, the fourth floor had turned into Grand Central Station, with the hustle and bustle of a fully occupied office complex. This sucked big time!

Sherry and I came out of the office to find ten of the investigators milling about, exploring offices and tinkering with their devices. Among the investigators was the owners' daughter (who managed the salon) and one of her friends, who came along for the ride. It was clear that, despite being very anxious, the daughter was trying to overcome her fear of the vacant spaces and whatever was taking place in the building.

Since the floor had been overrun, getting credible audio was out of the question. Instead, Sherry and I spoke with the daughter, asking about her experiences in the building. She explained that since the building totally creeped her out, she didn't spend a lot of time out of the storefront retail spaces. Though these upper floors were pretty bad, she thought the basement was the absolute worst.

"Have you ever been touched by an entity or had your hair pulled?" Sherry asked.

Uh oh, I thought. I didn't like where this was going.

No, the daughter answered, nothing ever physical, just glimpses of moving shadows and disconnected voices.

"You shouldn't be afraid of them," Sherry gently explained. "Think of them as people who are trapped."

A knot formed in my stomach.

"Do you believe in God?" Sherry continued.

The knot tightened.

"I'm Catholic," replied the daughter.

"I'm a Seventh Day Adventist," Sherry replied.

And I'm going to puke, I thought as I gently extricated myself from the conversation, reminding myself all the while that this was not my gig and these were not my people. I had reached a pivotal point in my young investigating career.

I was furious; I was angry with Big City Paranormal, I was angry with Bob, and I was particularly angry with myself for lowering my standards simply for the opportunity to possibly experience the paranormal. Though both these teams promote themselves as serious investigators, the truth of the matter is, neither had a clue. The last straw came as the investigation wound down and the remaining team members were preparing to depart.

Apparently, Bob had played back his audio recorder from one of his sessions and caught something. What it was, I don't know and I didn't want to know. Like a kid at Christmas, Bob rushed around the shop, playing and replaying the audio to everyone whether they wanted to hear it or not. One such bystander was the building's owner, who had an unabashed look of terror on her face. This was the worst possible outcome to the worst investigation I had ever experienced. To even call it an investigation is an insult. This wasn't an investigation; it was a debacle. If anything it was a ghost party, minus the beer and chips.

Why was this investigation a fiasco? First, it was poorly organized with little to no consideration given to the owners of the property and the number of participants who would, could, or should attend. Though we had permission to enter and explore the premises, nobody gave a thought beyond the *getting permission* part. It was like those high school days when your folks are out of town for the weekend and allow you to have a couple of friends over. Next thing you know, fifty uninvited people are trampling through your house.

Second, investigators have no business sharing their personal beliefs with the client, especially during the actual investigation. If you're going to call yourself an investigator, then behave like an investigator; keep your beliefs to yourself, and let the facts and evidence lead you to a finding. Your beliefs about the existence of spirits, ghosts, paranormal phenomena, and their relationship to God and religion are, in my opinion, irrelevant to the execution of an investigation. In fact, when you bring these beliefs into a formalized investigation, you compromise objectivity.

This is not a slight against God, religion, spiritualism, or people of faith. In my opinion, investigations and belief systems are mutually exclusive, meaning they are completely separate from each other. An investigation is simply the objective process and methodology of collecting data; that's it, nothing more. Simply put, if you go into an investigation with your biases and beliefs displayed on your sleeve, chances are pretty high you will find exactly what you're looking for. And it doesn't take a rocket scientist or research scholar to know this is bad method, bad process, and bad science.

Third and finally, you never share what I call the raw data (audio or video) with a client. Unless they are actively involved in the investigation and experience something with you or in your immediate presence, data should be thoroughly viewed and reviewed before your findings are made. Bob's zeal to share his data eclipsed the interests and sensitivities of the owner who invited us in. It was also really bad form and (in my opinion) very unprofessional. I promptly departed Bob's group and vowed never to participate in such a hack endeavor again.

Though I made a hasty departure from Bob's group, I must also give thanks and credit where it is due; my experiences with Bob and his group represent the true foundations of this book. Since he never pursued or inquired into my departure and I never offered anything more than a benign and courteous resignation, I didn't feel a discussion concerning the particulars would serve much purpose. Bob's group is Bob's group, and he has every right to operate the club he founded in any manner he sees fit.

The moral of this part of the story, especially to readers and enthusiasts who are unfamiliar with the hands-on practical aspects of paranormal investigating, is this: there really are no rules that guide or govern research societies and investigative teams. Anybody can call themselves an investigator, and anybody can create a web page to promote themself. Anybody can have business cards made, and anybody can hobble together a kit of cameras, gadgets, and gizmos that give the appearance they know what they're doing. The simple fact remains, all groups are *not* equal.

Is this important, and does it matter? I certainly think so, particularly when people invite you into their home or business looking for help, answers, and validation. Though I don't presume anything I write here is going to make a great deal of difference to some paranormal groups, I do think those who take this field seriously and consider themselves serious investigators have a responsibility to raise and maintain the highest level of quality in their standards and practices. If you are an investigator, then understand what it is to be an investigator, and act like one. If you're a thrill-seeker and ghost hunt for the fun and excitement, hey man, go for it! Be safe and have a ball. In either case, have the intellectual honesty to know and admit which of the two groups you belong to.

Prospect Place Manor

Thankfully, I've had many more positive experiences than negative ones, and my next C-Bus investigation proved to be one of the strangest experiences I've had to date. It took place in mid-November 2012 at the Prospect Place Manor in Trinway, Ohio. To those who are avid followers of paranormal TV programs, Prospect Place is very well known, perhaps even notorious. Built in 1856 by prominent landowner and abolitionist George W. Adams, Prospect Place was an important stop along the Underground Railroad.

Like so many haunted homes and buildings, the story of Prospect Place reveals a history of sorrows and suffering, punctuated by schemers and ne'er-do-wells such as the bricklayer who torched the mansion once it was finished just to keep working. Then there was the deadbeat son-in-law who one day simply vanished, abandoning wife and child to seek his fortunes in San Francisco. There are also the human suffering and tragedies associated with the pre–Civil War years, when fugitive slaves sought fleeting moments of warmth, safety, and scraps of food in their unimaginable odysseys of freedom. There were the deaths of loved ones over the years, even a 1912 train wreck that turned Prospect Place into a field hospital of sorts, where the injured were brought and triaged, and the dead were housed until next of kin could reclaim them.

Of course, legend and rumors also cloak the mansion—so much so that it can be difficult to distinguish fact from fiction. By now, you know I'm not a keen believer of legends, myths, and rumors. To me, it's all circumstantial hearsay . . . even if the stories are more than one hundred years old. I do, however, draw a distinction between the rumors and legends of places like "Mentor's Most Haunted" and the Prospect Place mansion. At Mentor's nature preserve, there were no clues or artifacts that directly connected the ghost stories with a historical context. Conversely, Prospect Place, like the Madison Seminary, is itself an artifact. Coupled with the treasure trove of materials and archival evidence collected over the years, its stories certainly present a far more plausible, if not researchable, case in support of its legends, circumstantial though they may be.

Reprint courtesy of George Adams.

Three of Prospect Place's more renowned legends that directly relate to the paranormal are worthy of note; the first originates from the Civil War era, the second from the early twentieth century when the estate fell into decline, and the third legend from much more modern times.

The first legend involves the hanging of a bounty hunter who, under the auspices of the Fugitive Slave Act of 1850, came to the area in search of runaway slaves who could be captured and returned to their owners for big money profits. According to the legend, occupants and perhaps neighbors of Prospect Place turned the tables on the mercenary, and the hunter became the hunted. Though the details are sketchy, as is common with legends, a kangaroo court was convened and vigilante justice quickly dispensed . . . at the end of a rope from the rafters of Prospect Place's barn.

The second legend surrounds the turn-of-the-century death of a female child at the mansion. There are two variants of this story, namely regarding the child's identity. The first suggests the girl was Constance Cox, the adopted daughter of Anna Adams-Cox (eldest daughter of G. W. Adams) and William Cox, Jr., the deadbeat dad who skipped out on his family. The second variant of the story identifies the child simply as a servant girl. Regardless of her identity, according to the legend, while in the delirium of a fever, the girl wandered onto a second-floor balcony and fell to her death. Since burial could not take place until the spring, the body was kept in the frigid basement until the ground warmed and a proper funeral could take place; this was a common practice of the period. In the version that identifies the girl as Constance, it is said that Anna sat a daily vigil with her deceased daughter until spring and the funeral, compounding her heartbreak and already fragile condition.

The final, more recent legend of interest is also based within a historically plausible context. Back in the 1960s and '70s, when the mansion was vacant and bouncing between investors, vandals broke in, defacing and destroying much of the structure's interior. During this period, a group of Satanists *supposedly* conducted rituals in the third-floor ballroom. One of these *supposed* rituals involved black magic and the conjuring of a demon, which *supposedly* still resides there, taunting and occasionally lashing out at investigators.

These fanciful tales certainly make for good television, as has often been the case with the para-celebs who have come with their production teams to create their made-for-TV entertainment. Regardless of my beliefs and perspective, I also recognize that I don't live in a bubble, and I am not immune to the influences these paranormal TV programs have on viewers and investigators. This made my mid-November investigation of Prospect Place Manor all the more compelling.

Though I'm leery of the legends, there's something about Prospect Place that brings these ethereal fictions strikingly to earth, especially when you finally reach Trinway and pull into the drive for the first time. Of all the mansion-style homes I've investigated to date, none exudes the look and feel of a classic haunted house more than Prospect Place.

When we arrived at Prospect Place, we were warmly greeted by George Jeffrey Adams, great-great-grandson of the original G. W. Adams. George is an interesting fellow characterized by some in the paranormal community as being cool and aloof. This was not my experience. As geeks of a feather with mutual interests in history, archaeology, and academia, we got along well, spending a good hour chatting about our shared interests. I learned that George was highly educated, and during his college years he even participated in an archaeological dig at Luxor, Egypt. This created a natural transition to the archaeological digging I've done in central Ohio and the focus of my undergraduate and graduate studies—which brought us right back to Prospect Place itself, a parcel within a region that has been inhabited for literally thousands of years.

As the conversation returned to the present and our investigation, George became more reserved, stating that he didn't like to have lengthy discussions about the paranormal and the phenomena occurring at Prospect Place. Though he has an excellent relationship with the greater paranormal community, whose interest and support has enabled him to undertake the massive structural rehabilitation under way while operating the (nonprofit) G. W. Adams Education Center at Prospect Place, he had also been stung by some of the paranormal celebrities and their producers who have investigated the mansion.

I respect and appreciate George's perspective. Although he readily admits to strange goings-on in the mansion, he explains that people need to experience Prospect Place for themselves and on their own terms, and that the last thing any investigation needs is an overzealous docent filling a team with *supposedlys,* or leading them about or shadowing their every move.

Since this was C-Bus's third visit to Prospect Place in as many years, we bypassed the owner-guided tour; John knew this place almost as well as George. So with the formalities of fees, waivers, and pleasantries dispensed with, George bid us a good night and retired to his adjacent suite, leaving us to our task of wiring the mansion's three floors and basement for video and audio. The crew was thankfully small—comprised only of John, Mike Hale (C-Bus's former technical manager), and myself. A three-man crew and George, four men in the house—an important footnote to the evidence you will later hear.

Unlike my experience at Madison Seminary, where I was first learning to overcome my fear of the dark, I dug right into the setup. That doesn't mean I wasn't anxious. To the contrary, I was *very* anxious. Though the seminary has its devoted regional following and a growing reputation in the paranormal world,

Prospect Place is an iconic national gem, due in large measure to its popularization on TV. Although not as large as the seminary, or as expansive as the prisons, sanitariums, and asylums I would later investigate, Prospect Place is still a big-league player in America's Most Haunted.

After a team walk-through during which John and Mike gave locations and context to different pieces of evidence that had been collected in the past, we returned to the first-floor dining room and got to work with the setup . . . and the weirdness immediately began. Banging in the front parlor and heavy footsteps on the second floor gave John a good laugh. "Okay," he chuckled. "We're coming," he told our unseen hosts, as he pulled the DVR and monitor from their boxes.

While John was getting a laugh, I was struggling to keep a grip. Up until this point, I had never experienced anything like this before—that is, walking into a place and suddenly finding myself surrounded by audible paranormal activity. It was unnerving, but very cool. However unnerved I might have been, though, there were still cameras to set and cables to unwind, and the house was already dark. So with flashlight in my teeth, a roll of duct tape around my wrist, and what seemed liked miles of cable, I overcame the creep factor and did my job, feeding and securing hundreds of feet of cable throughout the four levels of the mansion.

As noted, Prospect Place was built in 1856 by George W. Adams, an ardent unionist, abolitionist, and twice-married man with a total of ten children. After his death in 1879, Prospect Place was bequeathed to his eldest daughter, Anna Adams-Cox, whose husband (the aforementioned William Cox, Jr.) is believed to have squandered Anna's inheritance, then skipped out on his wife and child. As you can imagine, William's mysterious departure quickly became the center of gossip and speculation for this small town.

George W. Adams

A family photograph from the 1890s taken in the Prospect Place library.
Top row from left: George Cox, William Cox, Jr., Unknown child,
Anna Adams-Cox and Unknown child. Second Row from left: Unknown woman,
Mrs. William Cox, Sr., Mary J. Robinson-Adams, Unknown woman.
Bottom Row: Sophia Adams, Unknown woman. Reprints courtesy of
George Adams.

William's disappearance, which was remarkably well documented by the local press at the time, reads like a modern-day soap opera—very modern-day. Eyewitness accounts later reported William first in Columbus, Ohio, and then in San Francisco, both times in the company of what witnesses report as "a strange man." Was William Cox, Jr. gay? It's anybody's guess, but it certainly adds an interesting twist to an early-1900s mystery. It is believed William Jr. met his demise during the great San Francisco earthquake and fire of 1906.

William's sudden and mysterious departure was a devastating blow to Anna, who never recovered, never remarried, and remained at Prospect Place along with her younger sister Mary, who also never married. The struggle to maintain the estate was a tremendous burden to a now heartbroken Anna. It is at this point in Prospect Place's chronology, after William's mysterious departure, that the story of a child dying in the house appears in the paranormal folklore.*

In the autumn of 1924, Anna fell on the ice and was seriously injured. She was at once returned to her beloved Prospect Place, where complications from the fall would take a further toll. On November 28, 1924, destitute, lonely, and still heartbroken over her many losses, Anna died in the house, and the already decaying Prospect Place fell into ruin. How sad and tragic for such a proud and noble family and their grand estate.

Fast-forward almost 100 years to the present and the heroic efforts of George J. Adams, heir to a rich name and legacy, who works tirelessly to restore the mansion to its original grandeur.

---

* *Though historical society records indicate Anna and William had a son (George), there is no record of an adoption, before or after William's disappearance. Additionally, there is no record or newspaper account of a girl dying at the estate during this same period.*

With our equipment set up, we began our investigation, beginning in the first-floor parlor, where we paid our respects to a portrait of G. W. Adams that proudly graces the fireplace mantle. From the parlor we advanced through the library, which has been converted into a small museum, displaying artifacts and documents from the building's past. From there, we ascended to the second-floor bedroom level, arguably the most active floor of the house, where we ultimately spent the lion's share of our investigating time. Similar to our experience when we first began our setup, the second floor also seemed to come alive, with whispering and footsteps in the hall.

We began in the master suite, where portraits of Mary (G. W.'s second wife) and Anna Cox-Adams hang. The air was heavy, and though we knew we were in the company of spirits, the room was deathly silent. We respectfully introduced ourselves and encouraged any of the spirits to communicate and interact with us: tug our sleeves, tap our shoulders, or touch our hands. We heard and felt nothing.

After thirty minutes, we advanced to the next bedroom, a much larger room where six beds gave the impression that it could very well have been used as a children's room during the mansion's early days. I had one strange personal experience in the room, which in hindsight leads me to believe I was literally touched by a playful spirit. As we prepared to move on, I felt a distinct tugging on the cuff of my pant leg. At first I thought I had snagged something—a string or length of video cable— and suddenly found myself doing a funky little chicken dance, scratching at the floor with my foot, trying to free myself from whatever I got caught on.

As an investigator, I've come to appreciate and to be more aware of these subtle, almost imperceptible little feelings, sensations, experiences. Experienced investigators frequently report a variety of physical sensations or experiences; most common are hair tugs, hand or arm touches, pokes, and even pushes, as Andrew experienced at the seminary. These types of sensations can be difficult to imagine, especially for folks who have never participated in an investigation. Of course, pushes and pokes are pretty obvious and relatively easy to feel and describe. If paranormally related, they represent pretty strong evidence of a spirit with something on his or her mind. The more subtle innocuous contacts are like walking under or brushing against a cobweb: very soft, very subtle, but very real.

After spending more than an hour on the second floor, the team returned to the first-floor dining room that served as headquarters. It was during this break, while the three of us were casually conversing, that one of our remote voice recorders picked up the most disturbing EVP of the evening. Though adjectives seldom fail me, I'm at a loss to describe it. Clearly human, the sound could be described as a groan, similar to the sound one might make when tasting something totally disgusting. In this audio clip, you can hear me jabbering away in the background. Who or what produced this EVP, and why, remains a mystery.

bit.ly/ghostlyencounters-prospect

I must confess, the most terrifying part of the night for me was when John sent me up to the third-floor ballroom by myself, to conduct a solo EVP session. This is where, *supposedly,* Satanists had performed their rituals and conjured a demon.

Legends aside, it is one thing to read or write about this stuff, and another thing altogether to be sitting alone in the dark where a *supposed* demon exists. As dubious or even skeptical as we might be of these tales and legends, we are nonetheless influenced by them, knowing that all such tales are in some small way rooted in fact. Of course, my question that night and in that space was: what part of this legend is real? With nothing but a flashlight, voice recorder, and walkie-talkie, I tried to get *something* to communicate with me. I lasted a whole seven and a half minutes.

Though I chuckle and blush with this confession, I feel compelled to also explain that it wasn't just the freak-factor of being alone in the dark that had me dashing out of the ballroom in under ten minutes. It was also a message over the walkie-talkie from tech manager Mike, who was dutifully watching the monitor in HQ and sent the following message.

bit.ly/ghostlyencounters-prospect

Momma didn't raise no fool, and when informed that an unseen "something" was behind me, logic and reason folded like a cheap suit. As you can see, when the fight-or-flight instinct kicked in, I opted to run!

After my experience in the ballroom, the house became extremely quiet, at least compared with the earlier part of the investigation. Though we did spend time out in the barn, where the bounty hunter was supposedly hanged, and conducted multiple sessions in the basement, where runaway slaves took refuge and the bodies of the deceased were sometimes kept, the frigid November night kept the outdoor sessions relatively short, and the hum and dust activity caused by a new boiler system made data collection in the basement virtually impossible.

For the final portion of the investigation, we conducted another series of solo sessions. Having had my fill of the ballroom, I returned to the large six-bed "children's room" I had investigated earlier. Hoping to encourage the spirit of the little girl to communicate with me, I used the same strategy that proved so effective at the seminary: I read to her. The results were astounding.

bit.ly/ghostlyencounters-prospect

Despite the temperature challenges we experienced in the barn and the mechanical obstacles in the basement, the team still had a remarkable experience. As you are about to hear, the ghosts of Prospect Place readily made their presence known. These are the bits of evidence obtained from our November 2012 investigation.

bit.ly/ghostlyencounters-prospect

Based on our evidence: (1) Prospect Place is indeed paranormally active; (2) there are two, possibly even three female spirits and at least one male spirit that made their presence known; and (3) there was no evidence obtained during this investigation that supports the presence of a bounty hunter in the barn or a demon in the ballroom.

Ohio State Reformatory

It was December 21, 2012, the end of the world . . . at least according to the dimwits who knew nothing about the Mayan calendar. On this blustery winter night, I would join the C–Bus team on a public investigation billed as an *extreme* paranormal investigation at the Ohio State Reformatory, in Mansfield, Ohio. And extreme it was!

Copyright © by Libby Zay.

Built in 1896 and operated until 1990, the Ohio State Reformatory (commonly referred to as OSR or Mansfield Reformatory) was a medium-security prison facility operated by the state of Ohio. Contrary to popular belief (and my own, until I educated myself about the prison's past), there was never a death row at OSR. Though some serious badasses served their time there, the worse of the worst were housed and/or executed at other Ohio maximum-security prisons.

Made famous in *The Shawshank Redemption,* a few scenes from *Air Force One,* and several music videos, OSR takes the creep factor to a whole new level. Despite its classification as a medium-security facility, this place exudes badness.

Unlike other paranormal hot spots with sketchy backgrounds, OSR possesses incredible historical context. Everything from the inmates who served their sentences to specific acts of violence are documented and archived here. Though legends do exist within these cold, foreboding walls, the truth is just as horrific as any myth or legend the imagination can conjure, such as the cold-blooded murder of two prison guards, one in 1926 and the other in 1932. Inmate suicides were also common, the most renowned being inmate Lockhart, who stole a small quantity of turpentine from the prison workshop, then set himself ablaze in his cell. It certainly makes you wonder: if this is what life was like in a medium-security facility, what hellish torments took place at a maximum-security center?

These facilities are a stark, unvarnished reflection of late nineteenth-and twentieth-century societal views toward crime and punishment. Though created with the best of intentions, time and indifference would grind these institutions into hellholes that were overcrowded, understaffed, inhumane warehouses of society's dregs, where violence was as much a part of the daily routine as the rats and cockroaches that shared inmate space.

The Ohio State Reformatory is truly an intimidating edifice and structure that I'm certain struck fear in most of the 115,000 men who served their time there during its functioning lifetime.

Investigating this behemoth would present unimaginable technical challenges that, as a novice, I simply couldn't even fathom. In fact, conducting an investigation of a facility of this size and scale is beyond most vocational investigators. I would further guess that to effectively cover OSR's two main cell blocks, four extensions, the administrative center, and countless work areas would challenge the largest, best-equipped Hollywood production companies.

Thankfully, I wasn't the one running the show, and John had no intention of treating this place like any of the other venues we had explored. This investigation would be a mobile event. In other words, if we couldn't carry it, we wouldn't use it. As such, we loaded up a backpack with the essential night-vision video gear: the parabolic microphone, headphones, digital cameras, and several voice recorders.

Along with sixty-five other extreme ghost hunters, we entered the storied reformatory, signed the waiver, briefly explored the welcome area/museum, and then entered the frigid dark. To be honest, I was a little concerned that, like the salon, sixty-four other participants traipsing around the prison and climbing around the massive cell blocks would contaminate our audio. John put my mind at rest. Sure, he admitted, we would certainly cross paths with various groups throughout the event, but the sheer size of the place would absorb this paltry handful of people. Audio shouldn't be a problem, he concluded, assuming people kept their wits and knew how to behave. Knowing how to behave meant keeping the chit chat to a minimum and not whispering or speaking in hushed tones when you did talk.

The crowd joining us that night was an interesting mix of enthusiasts and established investigators, with an equal mix of locals and out-of-towners. I myself had driven about an hour and a half from my northeast Ohio, lakeshore community. Other participants had traveled from as far as northern Michigan, central Indiana, and Pennsylvania to take part in this extreme event. Though there were a few OSR veterans like John and

Andrew, many of the participants, like me, were first-timers at this location.

We were also extremely fortunate to have Ryan B. at our side that night. Besides being a member of the C-Bus Paranormal family, he is also a paramedic and active volunteer with the Mansfield Reformatory Preservation Society (MRPS), the nonprofit organization that owns, curates, and administers this National Historic Landmark. Ryan knew this place as well as anyone, and though he was working that night as an OSR volunteer, he would provide us access, insight, and knowledge only insiders possess. Hopefully, we wouldn't need to call upon his medical skills.

As the investigation began and volunteers led groups of participants for guided tours, we peeled away from the main body

with Ryan, wasting little time climbing the wrought iron spiral stairs that flanked the massive cell blocks. Climbing those tight stairs and walking the narrow cell block walkways was a harrowing experience. Though the original railing is about waist high and has since been reinforced with tall steel grating, it doesn't take a lot of imagination to realize how easily a pissed-off inmate could have done-in a guard or another inmate with little more than a quick shove from his locked

Copyright © by Libby Zay.

cell. Ryan, John, and Andrew seemed to maneuver about quite comfortably, but it was a white-knuckle ride for me.

Like Prospect Place, OSR is an iconic paranormal hot spot that has never failed to deliver evidence to the observant eye or ear. A year before my visit to OSR, John and the formative C-Bus team obtained intriguing video evidence while investigating the warden's office. Is it a spirit remnant, a residual apparition of the warden or his wife, both of whom died in the warden's suite at the facility? We will never know. But the phenomenon that was captured, rare video evidence, is quite remarkable.

http://bit.ly/ghostlyencounters-osr

The Ohio State Reformatory is without question a freaky place, and like all other paranormal hot spots, it must be viewed within its historical and cultural context. Little wonder the EVPs captured during the investigation were either calls for help or unambiguous taunts and curses. When places like OSR were operating, "you were either predator or prey," remarked an OSR volunteer on one paranormal TV show. It should therefore come as no surprise that the spirits that remain in the reformatory are likewise both tormentors and the tormented.

About halfway through the investigation, we found ourselves outside the bull pen, a common area at the junction of the eastern and western cell blocks where investigators can sit down, warm up, eat some pizza, and relax a bit. While chatting with a couple who were describing a shadow they witnessed emerging from a sixth-floor cell, Andrew began complaining that the right side of his face was suddenly bothering him. Upon closer inspection with a flashlight, we watched as red scratch marks began forming.

As a material witness to the event, it was astonishing; at no point did Andrew touch his face or come in contact with anything. While we examined Andrew's face, John also suddenly reacted to . . . something. Passing the night camcorder to me, he gingerly touched the area around the corner of his left eye, which was profusely watering. Sure enough, his left lower eyelid was beginning to darken.

"What happened?" I asked.

"I feel like I got slapped," he replied flatly.

"Maybe we should move out of this area," Ryan suggested. "I don't know what you guys did, but someone's pissed off that you're here."

We returned to the bull pen and took a breather. Of course Andrew's face generated a lot of attention with the other folks in the area, and he unexpectedly found himself the center of attention and the subject of a lot of pictures. Clearly disturbed and a little rattled, John kept to himself. By the end of the investigation, John had a bona fide black eye.

The truth is, this type of physical interaction is common to investigators at OSR, though most common with folks who provoke the ghosts, which is not John's or Andrew's style. What I find striking (pardon the pun) is that I observed both events in real time, and neither Andrew nor John did anything to warrant the attacks. I'm equally curious why Ryan or I were not touched—maybe because I wear glasses and maybe because Ryan is a well-known volunteer, particularly among OSR's ghostly inhabitants? Your guess is as good as mine.

The subject of physical contact between entities and the living is highly controversial in the paranormal community. There are those who feel that without corroborating video evidence, such as a shadow literally coming in contact with someone and that contact captured on video, the experience does not qualify as evidence. On the other hand, there are those, especially some of the famous TV paranormal celebrities, who behave as if every unexplained skin irritation occurring in a haunted location has some kind of paranormal relationship. Though I tend to identify myself with the first group, I'm uncomfortable categorically disregarding these highly personal experiences as flukes or coincidences. That being said, here is the evidence obtained during my "End of the World" adventure at the Ohio State Reformatory.

http://bit.ly/ghostlyencounters-osr

As a writer and paranormal investigator, what truly fascinates me about places like OSR is the activity that continues and the entities that remain. It's easy to understand why the ladies of

Prospect Place would want to remain in their beloved home. But people like Lockhart, or the murdered guards from the 1926 and 1932 prison riots—why would these and countless, nameless others remain in such a dark and dismal place?

Though some believe these spirits linger because it's the only place they know or feel comfortable, still others suggest that many of these spirits don't even know they're dead—a concept that, at least for me, is difficult to comprehend. Regardless of what those reasons might be, here they remain . . . vaguely present in our world to those willing to listen.

Gettysburg

"I think the two greatest historic shrines in our country are both in Pennsylvania; Independence Hall and Gettysburg."
David McCullough, author/historian

It is estimated that between forty-six thousand and fifty thousand people were killed or wounded during this pivotal battle of the Civil War. Even at fifty-two years of age, I continue to be amazed by how the confluence of people, events, timing—and mistiming—came together to create a perfect storm of bloodshed and human slaughter. Although there are several equally horrific

battlefield sites across our great land which mark watershed moments in American history, few of them seem to touch the collective conscience like Gettysburg. Even 150 years later, the mere mention of Gettysburg still evokes a solemn reverence in all Americans, regardless of their background or state of origin.

It would be far too easy for me to slip into a digressive discussion on the background and significance of this defining moment of the war and our history. To those unfamiliar with the importance and intricacies of this battle, particularly younger readers who have yet to learn about its significance, I refer you to your local library or to any of several quality Internet sites devoted to the Civil War and the Battle of Gettysburg for a more thorough treatment on this truly epic battle.

Soaked in so much blood and tragedy, how could Gettysburg be anything but a nexus of paranormal activity? Even to those disinterested in the paranormal or outright skeptics, the ghosts of Gettysburg quietly resonate; it is truly hallowed ground. So when John, who had never been to and always wanted to experience Gettysburg, suggested a trip and investigation of the battlefield in early April 2013, I was first to sign up.

Since it was spring break for me, and John decided to take some vacation time off work, the adventure was expanded to include both the battlefield and an investigation of the Tillie Pierce House, a historic house (now a bed and breakfast) located on the south side of town, which saw periods of ferocious street-to-street fighting during the three-day battle. Having scheduled our visit early in the off-season, we were extremely fortunate to book all rooms in the B&B and thus have the entire location to ourselves. This would enable us to set up all our video equipment without concerns for or contamination from other guests.

For the first part of the trip—the battlefield—it would be John, Andrew, and me. Saturday, we would be joined by Julie and Mick, both huge fans of Gettysburg, who would meet us at the Tillie Pierce House. It was a perfect arrangement.

Unlike our previous investigation, the battlefields of Gettysburg presented some real logistical challenges, namely because they are outdoor sites located in a setting that is carefully monitored by the National Park Service (as it should be), and the park is a tourist magnet with throngs of tour buses and sightseers exploring it from morning to night. For those of you who have never been to Gettysburg, the Military Park covers an area of approximately fifteen square miles, crisscrossed with several paved roads specifically designed for self-guided auto tours, bus traffic, and parking. The park is free and open to the public, making it an extremely popular tourist destination, even in the off-season.

There's a reason why these sites were given names like the Bloody Wheatfield, Cemetery Ridge, and Devil's Den—the same reasons why people still flock to them today, and why the C-Bus team would also want to visit, with as much audio and video equipment as we could carry. The real investigative challenge would be trying to obtain as much raw audio and video data with as little contamination from other tourists as possible. Overcoming this obstacle made for a few *very* long days. Without special permits and access, the investigations would be restricted to the regular park hours, 6:00 a.m. to 10:00 p.m. We would be there to greet the sun at dawn and bid the ghosts peaceful repose at night.

The team arrived and assembled on a Thursday afternoon at a campground situated on the periphery of the park. As the old man of the group, I had insisted that the extent of me "roughing it" would be a heated cabin. Though clean sheets and room service would have been nice, I could take one for the team and dig out the sleeping bag, which hadn't seen the light of day for twenty years. I also had to have coffee. Even as a very willing participant, I don't drag my butt anywhere, ghosts or no ghosts, especially at 6:00 a.m., without a hot cup of joe within easy reach. Of course, John promised to arrange the appropriate accommodations.

With our three-man team assembled, we went to explore the park, giving John and Andrew an opportunity to see the sites and monuments by day. Even though it was early April, the park was already overflowing with tour buses, caravans of cars, and license plates from virtually every state, all wanting to see places and monuments that have been burned into the American conscience.

On a more personal note, I feel compelled to mention that the Gettysburg experience has changed over the years since my first childhood visit. Though the park itself hasn't changed, it seems the visitors have—with a diminished sense of respect. Many people (pet owners and the parents of young children in particular) appear indifferent to many of the battlefield's landmark locations; Devil's Den is not a backyard jungle gym, and the walking paths are not dog-runs.

At Devil's Den, I was honestly appalled at how lax parents were with their children on this very dangerous geological formation, and how many pet owners brought their animals to a battlefield memorial. Why do people do this? Do they expect to picnic or play Frisbee with Fido on the fields where thousands died? Gettysburg is not a recreation area, it's a national shrine, where tens of thousands were killed and wounded. Although the National Park Service does an excellent job of maintaining and administering the site, I wish more could be done to instill and promote the reverence Gettysburg Military Park has earned.

Having walked and toured several of the locations throughout the park, we decided to leave and allow the crowds to thin. We then shifted our focus to an off-site landmark that has become quite popular in the paranormal community: Sachs Bridge.

Sachs Covered Bridge (formerly known as Sauck's Covered Bridge)—a Town's lattice truss bridge was originally built in 1854 and used by both armies, first by units of the Union First and Third Corps. After the start of the battle, the area surrounding Sachs Bridge quickly transformed into a Confederate encampment

and staging area for the two bloody days that followed. Records indicate the bridge was also used as a field hospital, and possibly the location where three Confederate deserters were hanged. Four days after the start of the battle, Robert E. Lee and the Army of Northern Virginia retreated south across the bridge,[2] eventually making it to Maryland and back to Virginia.

Sauck's (Sachs) Bridge

2   Zacher, Susan M (1980). "Sauck's (Sachs) Covered Bridge"

Like many of the sites off the beaten path, Sachs Bridge is a serene landmark that easily hides its history. Although many paranormal investigating teams have spent late night hours at the bridge and have recorded numerous EVPs and taken many ghost-image photographs, we were unsuccessful in our attempts to capture evidence of paranormal activity.

Our next investigative efforts began the following morning, promptly at 6:00 a.m., when rangers opened the parking area just beneath Devil's Den. Starting early proved to be an excellent strategy. With the exception of a single photographer waiting to snap pictures of the sunrise over Little Round Top, we had this section of battlefield all to ourselves.

From the parking area beneath Devil's Den, we followed a walking path that crossed the Plum Run (creek) into the tall grasses separating Big Round Top and Devil's Den, the southern flank of two Union lines and a location that came to be known as the Slaughter Pen: crucial piece of real estate that Union forces fought desperately to hold and Confederate forces struggled in vain to capture.

After an extensive audio and video session, we left the Slaughter Pen and walked the narrow valley northward, with

Houck's Ridge to our left and Little Round Top to our right, an area aptly named the Valley of Death, stopping frequently to reach out to the beleaguered spirits who might notice us. The quiet solitude of these places was both humbling and eerie—no cars, no buses, no people—only nature, and the knowledge that hundreds had fallen on this broken patch of earth, fighting for causes they believed in. From the Valley of Death and the base of Devil's Den, we then drove the short distance to the top of Little Round Top and watched the sun rise on this beautiful yet terrible place. By 7:30 a.m., the carloads of sightseers began trickling in, and our quality time in this section of the battlefield was over.

As you probably know, there are dozens if not hundreds of stories of people seeing apparitions and hearing the sounds of battle or the voices of the fallen on these bloodied fields. Even though I heard no musket fire and saw no ghosts, I knew deep in my heart that the team was not alone on that cold, clear morning.

From Little Round Top we moved to the Wheatfield, where we attempted to conduct additional audio and video sessions. Unfortunately for us, Gettysburg was waking up and a combination of local and tourist traffic made continued recording impossible. For the balance of the day, we blended into the crowds and explored other battlefield sites and locations within the town itself.

Though all of Gettysburg is truly historic, encompassing both the battle and President Lincoln's visit and dedication of the national cemetery, the town is generally composed of two basic areas: the southern part of town that includes most of the battlefield monuments, landmarks, and the kitsch tourist T-shirt shops (on Baltimore Street), and the northern "downtown" business district, where Lincoln arrived by railcar and overnighted (at the David Wills House) prior to the dedication.

Six years ago, when I brought my middle-school-aged son to Gettysburg for several days of exploration and explanations, there was only one outfit conducting ghost tours. Of course we attended, and it was . . . entertaining. Six years hence, and the ghost tours/paranormal investigating craze seems to have taken over the town, with walking tours and investigations available from every gift shop. To me, the endeavor is a double-edged sword. On the one hand, I appreciate how these ventures bring in much-needed revenue to Gettysburg, especially during these difficult economic times. On the other hand, I believe pay-to-play operations tend to distract and detract from efforts to advance the discussions in paranormal investigating. Personally, I believe there's a huge difference between sites and locations that charge admission to investigate and groups and organizations that charge people admission to observe or participate in an investigation; these situations are not equal.

We returned to the battlefields about 7:00 p.m., when twilight was fading into nightfall, and the buses and tourists had for the most part gone for the day. Though a few diehard tourists were finishing their rounds of the self-guided tours, the quiet and serenity we had experienced at dawn was slowly beginning to return. Of the entire Gettysburg adventure, nightfall in the Bloody Wheatfield was by far the eeriest. Some historians describe the fighting that took place there as the bloodiest and most chaotic of the entire Gettysburg campaign, with waves of assaults, offensives, counter-offensives, and flanking maneuvers that continue to astonish scholars and historians today. It is estimated that twenty thousand soldiers were involved in the fighting and six thousand were killed, wounded, or captured on these fields, prompting Civil War photographer Timothy O'Sullivan to name his now iconic photograph, taken at the Wheatfield, "Harvest of Death."

As the darkness surrounded us and the quiet closed in, we were distinctly aware that we were not alone. Unlike our early morning sessions in the Slaughter Pen beneath Devil's Den, and the Valley of Death under the shadow of Little Round Top, the vibe was completely different. Here in the Wheatfield, the air was heavy with an unseen yet palpable tension. We were all visibly anxious, keenly aware of a subtle energy gathering like the cold spring mist. On numerous occasions each of us would quickly turn, thinking we had heard a whisper or a footfall in the soft, compressed stubble of the thick grasses that now cover these killing fields, asking each other "Did you hear that?" After more than an hour of quietly traversing the Wheatfield and gently, respectfully encouraging the spirits of the dead to speak to us, we decided it was time to move on.

From the Wheatfield we drove approximately a mile and a half to the small cleft or saddle that separates Big Round Top and Little Round Top. During the war, this area represented the crucial flank of the Union forces, vigorously defended by the Twentieth Maine Infantry Regiment under the command of Col. Joshua Lawrence Chamberlain. This position was essential in the defense of Little Round Top and the Union line.

After taking Devil's Den on the second day of battle, Confederate forces proceeded to charge the Union flank, driving no less than three dramatic assaults into the saddle against Chamberlain's position; the losses were staggering.

Exhausted, out of ammunition, and knowing they could not withstand another assault, Private Theodore Gerrish of the Twentieth Maine Infantry recounted the actions that followed.

Our line was pressed back so far that our dead were within the lines of the enemy. Our ammunition was nearly all gone. We could remain as we were no longer: we must advance or retreat. [Col. Joshua Lawrence Chamberlain] understood how it could be done. "Fix bayonets" and the steel shanks of the bayonets rattled upon the rifle barrels. "Charge bayonets, charge!"

For a brief moment the order was not obeyed, and the little line seemed to quail. In that moment of supreme need Lt. H. S. Melcher, with a cheer and a flash of his sword, sprang full ten paces to the front, more than half the distance between the hostile lines. "Come on! Come on! Come on, boys!!" he shouted. With one wild yell of anguish wrung from its tortured heart, the regiment charged.

We struck the Rebels with a fearful shock. They recoiled, staggered, broke and ran, and like avenging demons our men pursued. The Rebels rushed toward a stone wall but to their surprise and ours, two scores of rifle barrels gleamed over the rocks, and a murderous volley was poured in upon them at close quarters. A band of men leaped over the wall and captured at least 100 prisoners.[3]

With the Confederate charge shattered, the Union positions on Little Round Top were saved, turning the tide of the Gettysburg campaign and making Joshua L. Chamberlain a Union hero for all time.

---

[3]   Gerrish, Theo. (1882) *A Private's Reminiscences of the Civil War.*

There, at that famous Union flank, we parked the car and armed ourselves with digital audio recorders and night-vision cameras. We then entered the hotly contested cleft between the two Round Tops, slowly walking west into the Valley of Death toward Devil's Den. Three days after the battle, looking upon this very scene from the heights of Little Round Top, Tillie Pierce (whose home we would be investigating the following night) wrote in her journal:

> As we stood upon those mighty boulders, and looked down into the chasms between, we beheld the dead lying there just as they had fallen during the struggle. From the summit of Little Round Top, surrounded by the wrecks of battle, we gazed upon the valley of death beneath. The view there spread out before us was terrible to contemplate! It was an awful spectacle! Dead soldiers, bloated horses, shattered cannon and caissons, thousands of small arms. In fact everything belonging to army equipments, was there in one confused and indescribable mass.[4]

As with the Bloody Wheatfield, the cold night air seemed heavy and charged. Adding to the strangeness of the uneasy quiet was the bright glow from the viewfinder of our night-vision camcorder, highlighting the sunbaked, rocky slopes that surrounded us. We wasted little time and began our investigation with polite introductions and gentle proclamations, explaining we meant no disrespect and wanted to listen and learn from anyone who would speak to us.

Time seemed to pass very quickly as we again slowly made our way through areas of the Slaughter Pen and throughout the Valley of Death. We did not realize it in the moment, but a few of Gettysburg's ghosts revealed themselves to us, answering our call and providing a stark and profound message.

---

[4]   Alleman, (Pierce) Tillie, *At Gettysburg, or What a Girl Saw and Heard of the Battle* (1888, reprinted 1994)

bit.ly/ghostlyencounters-gettysburg

Our time on the battlefield was drawing to a close. However, before departing for the night, I wanted to extend our investigation a little farther, onto ground generally off the common tourist path. Not far from where we parked, a worn footpath led across the southeastern backside of Little Round Top. This, I believe, would have been either the terminus of the Union left flank, where the Twentieth Maine Infantry and Joshua Chamberlain held fast to their position or at the very least an area where injured Union soldiers retreated from the field. Walking into the forested area and finding a quiet place, we settled in for our last session of the night.

It's impossible to say whether the knocks, creaks, clatter of stones, or steps through the brush were natural woodland sounds or of a paranormal nature. Making the assumption we were in the company of a spirit, John asked a very simple question . . . and received a profoundly simple response.

bit.ly/ghostlyencounters-gettysburg

There are countless myths that swirl around virtually every aspect of the Battle of Gettysburg. One such myth is that the Gettysburg campaign was the result of an accidental meeting of the two armies, when brigades of the Confederate army broke from the main force to maraud and plunder Gettysburg, searching for food and supplies. Other records indicate that General George Meade, commander of the Army of the Potomac, was in fact planning on a major engagement with Lee's Army of Northern Virginia. Lee's bold advance north out of Virginia into Maryland and Pennsylvania, the second since the onset of the war (the first taking place at Sharpsburg, Maryland, and the Battle of Antietam), represented the gravest of threats to the Union cause. Lee believed if he could capture Baltimore, or better still Philadelphia, northern politicians would have little choice other than to sue for peace and end the conflict. Of course, President Lincoln would have none of it.

As a student of history, it's fascinating to observe that despite possessing superior numbers and resources, the Union army was still rather clumsy, often slow to act or react to Lee's audacious tactics and strategies. I don't believe it takes a Civil War scholar to observe that while General Lee aggressively prosecuted the war, the Union response, especially in the early years, might be described as passively defensive. One need only examine a basic battlefield map and observe the obvious to appreciate the brilliance of Robert E. Lee's generalcy. In every engagement of the war, at least until Gettysburg, the Union army was chasing after, defending against, or retreating from Lee's smaller force—in other words, reacting or responding to Lee's movements and tactics. In the days preceding the Battle of Gettysburg, Lee's Army of Northern Virginia effectively hid from and outflanked the Army of the Potomac, coming north out of Virginia on the western side of town before wheeling east, taking Gettysburg from the north and west. How strangely ironic: the army of the South would engage their enemy from the north, and the Northern army would mount their defenses from the south.

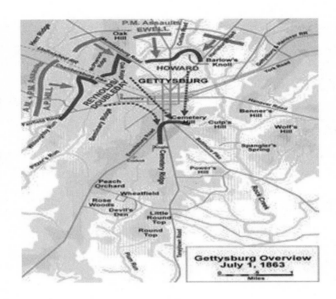

Map by Hal Jespersen.

As the map of the first day of battle illustrates, and the engagements that took place on the second day at the Wheatfield, Devil's Den, and Little Round Top indicate (where our initial paranormal investigations took place), fighting was intense and fast, moving with the Army of Northern Virginia sweeping south–southeast, pushing the Union army back through the town proper into the southern countryside.

In a sort of reverse chronological order, the second part of our Gettysburg adventure brought us into town, for a night at the Tillie Pierce House Bed & Breakfast, where the tide of battle first swept over the town. Though the house and landmark are named for Tillie, the home actually belonged to Tillie's parents, James and Margaret Pierce, at the time. He was a prominent local businessman and she was a housewife and mother.

Rumors abounded of the battle, but exactly when and where the armies would engage was anybody's guess. On that fateful first day of July 1863, the memories of a fifteen–year–old girl would capture the attention of the nation, drawing it to the drama that literally exploded around her.

Tillie Pierce (top left). A "then and now" of the Tillie Pierce House, at Baltimore & Breckenridge Streets.

Tillie, whose diary and accounts would later become a crucial record of the battle, was herself sent away from the house at the onset of fighting. Hoping to protect their daughter, James and Margaret sent Tillie with their neighbor, Henrietta Shriver and her two daughters, to take refuge at Henrietta's father's (Jacob Weikert) farm, three miles south of town. However, rather than escaping the approaching battle, Tillie found herself in the eye of the storm, as Weikert's farmhouse was less than a mile east of Little Round Top.

Truly, none could escape the collision of the two armies. While Tillie provided what aid and comfort she could to the wounded and dying at Weikert's farm, her parents' neighborhood witnessed a different kind of battle: street-to-street urban fighting. And while the Pierces and other citizens took in injured Union soldiers and in a few cases hid officers from Confederate capture, two doors down from Tillie's home, Confederate sharpshooters took up positions on the second floor of Henrietta Shriver's home, picking off Union officers and raining death upon unsuspecting soldiers.

After extensive remodeling and renovations, the Tillie Pierce House reopened for business in August 2011, providing its guests comfortable, modern amenities in a beautiful period theme. Antiques, period-style furnishings, and decorative accessories took the C-Bus team back to the mid-1800s when James Pierce was a successful butcher who operated his business on the first floor, with the family's domicile on the second.

At the onset of the battle, James's daughter, Matilda Jane (Tillie), then fifteen years old, attended the Young Ladies Seminary at the Gettysburg Female Institute. On June 26th, 1863, the dark clouds and rumble of the approaching storm blackened the horizon. Tillie recounted:

> We were having our literary exercises on Friday afternoon, at our Seminary, when the cry reached our ears. Rushing to the door, and standing on the front portico we beheld in the direction of the Theological Seminary, a dark, dense mass, moving toward town. Our teacher, Mrs. Eyster, at once said: 'Children, run home as quickly as you can.'
>
> It did not require repeating. I am satisfied some of the girls did not reach their homes before the Rebels were in the streets.
>
> As for myself, I had scarcely reached the front door, when, on looking up the street, I saw some of the men on horseback. I scrambled in, slammed shut the door, and hastening to the sitting room, peeped out between the shutters.
>
> What a horrible sight! There they were, human beings! Clad almost in rags, covered with dust, riding wildly, pell-mell down the hill toward our home! Shouting, yelling most

unearthly, cursing, brandishing their revolvers, and firing left and right."[5]

We arrived at Tillie Pierce House in the middle afternoon and were met by innkeeper Greg Christiansen. Affable and extremely knowledgeable, Greg warmly welcomed us into the beautifully appointed inn, giving us a detailed tour, including the paranormal hot spots. He explained that the most common activity was footsteps in the attic at all hours (day and night), room and dresser doors that opened and closed on their own, audible mumbles and whispers, and the mewing of a cat; there were no resident cats on the premises. He also noted that one of the most consistent reports from guests staying at the inn was an exceptionally loud bang that occurred at 3:00 a.m. Greg likened it to the sound of a heavy box or piece of furniture falling on the attic floor.

This would indeed be a fun case . . . and a tenfold upgrade from the shoebox cabin of the two previous nights. We could investigate at our leisure and when tired, get a good night's sleep while allowing our equipment to run nonstop and unimpeded until morning. Since we had the whole of the inn to ourselves that night, we were encouraged to explore and investigate all the accessible rooms and closets. Our only restrictions were Greg's office, the attic, and unfortunately, the basement, where James and Margaret sheltered during the days of battle and successfully hid several injured Union soldiers. According to Greg, ongoing renovations had temporarily turned the basement into a construction zone and until the work was complete, visitors and guests were prohibited from access.

After picking our rooms and unloading the vehicles, Greg gave us the keys to the inn, his emergency phone number, and best wishes on a successful investigation. He departed for the

---

[5] Alleman, (Pierce) Tillie, *At Gettysburg, or What a Girl Saw and Heard of the Battle* (1888, reprinted 1994)

night shortly thereafter. We immediately proceeded with the setup. Compared to many of the other locations, wiring the inn was a piece of cake. With an IR camera in each room trained on specific areas, there remained ample equipment and cable to cover the hallways, stairways, and attic. In about forty minutes, we were set to go . . . thus enabling the grungiest of us to clean up, rest up, and catch a decent meal.

We began recording audio and video once the DVR system was wired, but did not begin the formal investigating until almost 10:00 p.m. Even though we were visiting during the last weeks of the official off-season, Gettysburg, particularly during the 150th anniversary year, was vibrant and full of people. Many of the outfits that offer ghost tours were fully operational, conducting two tours per night for groups of fifteen to twenty-five people each. Of course, Tillie Pierce House is a prominent stop on each of these tours, and between the hours of 8:00 p.m. and 11:00 p.m., the outside of the inn was frequently visited by large groups of people taking part in the walking tours. Naturally, we had our own fun, occasionally stepping out the front door with our cameras, filming the delighted sightseers who were filming their tour and then filming us.

As for the evidence collected, Tillie Pierce House provided a few bits of curious and interesting audio evidence, as you will soon hear. They are, unfortunately, marginal at best, at least when compared to other haunted locations or even the battlefields themselves. These are the audio clips captured during our investigation at Tillie Pierce House, Gettysburg, Pennsylvania, April 2013.

bit.ly/ghostlyencounters-tillie

Regardless of whether you're a history geek or not, Gettysburg will always be a historic Mecca for young and old, scholar and novice. In the immortal words of Abraham Lincoln, "The world will little note, nor long remember what we say here, but it can never forget what they did here." This idea, this belief, so eloquently articulated by perhaps our most beloved president, again resonates deeply in my heart and mind, prompted by the ghost of a soldier—who, on a cold spring night on a now-peaceful field of battle, whispered "Remember."

4

Gizmos and Gadgets: A Cautionary Tale

At the beginning of our journey, we discussed the importance of having reliable equipment to document your findings during an investigation. Each team will eventually develop their own foundation of what works and what doesn't for their method of collecting evidence. It's important to have an arsenal of equipment at your disposal, but it's equally important to avoid the marketing gimmicks behind some of the flashier gizmos available.

Perceptions of the paranormal investigation field have changed greatly over the past decade or so, most of which can be attributed to the influx of paranormal reality shows currently on television. It's no longer taboo to want to explore the unknown, and merchants are lining up in droves to create the latest in ghost hunting technology. Séances, dowsing rods, Ouija boards, and table tipping have become relics of the past, and it's important that we look to the future in our attempt to prove the existence of life after death.

Have we made any recent progress with modern technology, or is the paranormal field being cluttered with more unproven products in the name of entertainment? Let's take a moment to review some of the more common devices currently available.

Electromagnetic Field (EMF) Meter:

 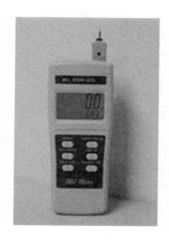 

The EMF meter is one of the most universal and controversial tools in the paranormal field today and is packaged under several different names (K2, Mel-meter, and more). Though it is widely believed that spirits are composed of electromagnetic energy that can be detected by these devices, it is important to remember that nearly everything in nature, both alive and inanimate, emits an electromagnetic field. Likewise, many man-made electrical devices and appliances, such as computers, televisions, refrigerators, fuse boxes, and even household electrical outlets also emit EMFs when functioning properly.

Originally designed for industrial electrical uses, EMF meters provide the user with a measurement (in the standard unit of measure, the milligauss) showing how high the electromagnetic field levels are within the range of the device, generally three to six feet. EMF "hits" or "spikes" are indicated by green or red LEDs that light up on the device. But the controversy surrounding this device is relatively unknown to many enthusiasts and novice users, and we have often seen other teams misuse or misinterpret an EMF meter.

It's important to remember that (1) EMF meters are very sensitive; and (2) EMF levels fluctuate—they're not constant. Take your average refrigerator, particularly an older model—though the appliance will give off a standard or baseline EMF reading (also known as a signature), its EMF will jump dramatically when the compressor kicks on or the icemaker engages. Some investigators are also unaware of just how much their other electronic devices can influence what an EMF meter is measuring. Everything from cell phones, battery-powered cameras, and two-way (walkie-talkie) radios to electrical wiring and cellular towers can generate false positives. These spikes often lead newer investigators to believe they're communicating with a spirit when they're actually not. Even on reality TV shows, you frequently see investigators attempt to communicate or believe they are communicating with a spirit based on EMF spikes.

Though interesting and even encouraging, especially when it appears an interaction is taking place between an investigator and an entity, there is usually a more logical explanation for an EMF fluctuation. This is why it is *very* important to be aware of your location and surroundings; this includes the building's physical location and proximity to things like cell towers or electrical substations, the presence of live machinery and/ or appliances in the building, even the general condition of electrical service in the location. Poorly insulated and jumbled wiring, and even strings of extension cords brought in by the investigators, can affect the EMFs in a room.

Though C-Bus Paranormal uses both the Mel and K2 meters during our investigations, we do not use these tools for spirit communication. Our team will normally perform a sweep of a location before an investigation begins to see where there might be high levels of electromagnetic energy already. Extended exposure to EMFs can cause problems that hamper investigations and in some cases may explain feelings of uneasiness or dread.

Electromagnetic (EM) Pump

The next device on our list is the EM Pump. This device is supposed to emit high levels of electromagnetic energy in an approximate ten-foot radius and is believed to energize spirits. *In theory,* spirits can use this energy to help them manifest visually and/or provide clearer audio responses. In other words, investigators who use the EM Pump believe that spirits can feed off the energy the device produces—an extension to the theory that spirits are made up of, emit, and require electromagnetic energy in order to manifest.

The EM Pump has become a rather popular device among paranormal investigators over the last few years, with various custom designs available online. Rather than test their luck with the quality issues common to the open market in an experimental field, innovative, cost-efficient investigators might even decide to research a unit's design and build one of their own. We've seen several different types of these devices that operate with varying degrees of reliability. Remember to exercise caution around high EMFs, and make sure to keep a safe distance away from the device when it's in full operation.

The Spirit Box

The spirit box is another device that carries several names (Ghost Box, Frank's Box [after the inventor], etc.) and is used in attempts to communicate with spirits through radio frequencies. The device itself is a receiver that cycles through the radio spectrum. It creates a barrier of white noise as it scans through the AM/FM stations. The theory behind this device is that spirits use the generated white noise as a medium to communicate with the living world.

The spirit box has become popular over the last few years and is routinely seen on most paranormal TV shows. But can it really communicate with spirits? Our team has field-tested a few of these devices throughout the years and found them to be incredibly inconsistent. There have only been a few times when we have received direct responses to questions we asked, or apparent comments made through the device that directly related to the case we were working on at the time. Most skeptics will tell you the device just provides a form of audio pareidolia—that the user will hear what they want to hear when trying to make sense of the chatter on the radio waves.

A new accessory recently added to our spirit box kit is the Faraday Cage, a grounded and specially treated pouch-like bag that shields the spirit box, eliminating voices or music of AM and FM radio signals. Though helpful in eliminating radio chatter, our tests have also been inconclusive using the Cage.

The concept behind the spirit box and other white-noise generators is intriguing, and although we tend to be skeptical of the responses it creates, we do manage to get some use out of it in all of our cases. If you're thinking of obtaining one of these devices, make sure to do your own research before taking the plunge. Obviously, a device that could actually communicate with the dead would represent a revolutionary breakthrough in the field of paranormal research. Throughout history, several great minds have attempted to achieve this feat, including Thomas Edison; but none has succeeded . . . yet.

The Ovilus

The Ovilus has been around for quite a few years now and is available in various versions. The device is similar to the spirit box in nature but does not rely on or function as a radio frequency scanner. Several paranormal theories suggest that spirits, whether they intend to or not, alter their environment in several ways, such as creating spikes in the ambient electromagnetic field or by causing temperature fluctuations—such as the sudden appearance of cold spots. The makers of the Ovilus claim that, by similarly manipulating its EM frequencies, a spirit can choose a specific response from a preset database of over two thousand words—in other words, that an intelligent entity will be able to alter the environment in such a way that it forces the Ovilus to "speak" an appropriate response to an investigator's question.

To be honest, we have yet to determine how the creators of this device came to believe that such a device could communicate with the dead, unless of course you're communicating with a tech savvy ghost. Can the Ovilus operate as advertised or does it just spit out random words that could relate to nearly any given situation? Your guess is as good as ours, but we're more than a little skeptical.

Some paranormal groups like this device and others avoid it completely. The important thing to remember about the Ovilus is that it's also advertised as being "for entertainment purposes only," and that entertainment comes at a steep price; these devices can cost a few hundred dollars. More recently, the *entertaining* concept of the Ovilus has been duplicated and is now available as a free cell phone application. Personally, our team doesn't use these devices, and we encourage every investigator to look at both device and app with a great deal of skepticism.

Parabolic Dish

The parabolic dish is a unique device that provides amplification of nearby sound waves—and in turn provides the investigator a chance to listen closely to ambient sound in real time. The device comes equipped with a built-in parabolic microphone that focuses sound waves from the reflector (or dish)

into the microphone's receiver, which is then patched into a set of headphones or recording device. This setup allows the user to listen to and record sounds from several meters away, and who wouldn't want to hear their audio evidence as it's being captured?

Like all special purpose tools, the parabolic dish has its limitations. Though it does provide enhanced real-time audio, it must also be closely aimed at the source of the sound or the specific area being investigated. Parabolic dishes also pick up *everything*, from the squeak of someone's shoes to the grumble of someone's stomach (which is always rather interesting), to a conversation on the opposite side of a room. The best solution to these problems is to practice using this device in a controlled indoor environment. The operators should then be able to improve their skill and success rate by limiting the amount of space they're attempting to cover. We routinely use the parabolic dish during investigations, and it's an excellent tool for investigators interested in real time audio.

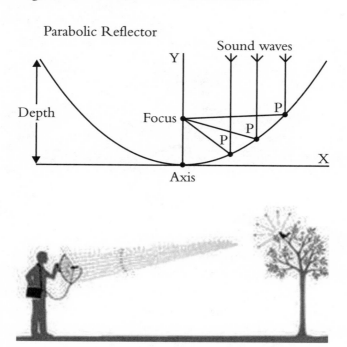

Parabolic Reflector

One final note on the parabolic dish. Though it works exceptionally well as a stand-alone tool, it does not necessarily work well with all digital voice/audio recorders, particularly if the user seeks to listen and record simultaneously. This is especially true with low-end voice recorders such as the RCA and Olympus models mentioned in the previous tech chapter. In the field, we get great results by patching the parabolic dish to our H1 Zoom recorder and then plugging our headphones into the recorder.

Laser Grid

The laser grid is probably the cheapest and most cost-effective way for paranormal investigators to attempt to document shadow movement within a location. The laser grid is normally set up on a tripod in a room where paranormal activity is believed to be at its peak. It's not uncommon to see the laser grid accompanied by a video camera to document any visual disturbance that might occur while the device is being used. The laser pen itself will project a grid of dots throughout the room, covering a significant area. Most investigators believe that spirits or shadow figures can manipulate or disrupt the diagram if they manifest or move across the grid itself during an investigation.

Buyers Beware: Many investigators purchase and attempt to use the popular "laser pen" model to document activity but are unaware that these models are not made for extended use. As the diode crystals within the laser begin to overheat (after approximately ten to fifteen minutes of continuous use), sections of the laser grid will start to fade out, giving a false impression that some type of phenomenon is taking place. There are plug-in lasers on the market that have internal cooling systems that don't overheat, but you can expect them to be larger and also more expensive. Exercise caution if you're planning to use any form of laser grid during an investigation, and be aware of its weaknesses and limitations.

Thermal Imaging Device

The thermal imaging device is one of the most sought-after pieces of equipment in the paranormal field today. Many investigators consider it the holy grail of paranormal research equipment and will save up thousands of dollars to purchase a unit to use in the field. However, the thermal imager can be a common source of false evidence if the user does not understand the device's capabilities, limitations, or correct usage.

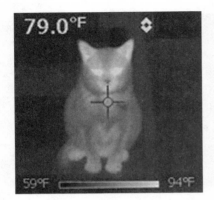
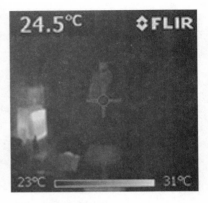
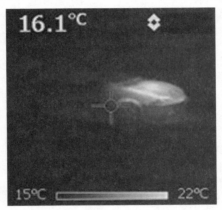

Thermal imaging devices (a.k.a. FLIR—Forward Looking Infrared Radiometer) use lenses and sensors to convert an object's infrared radiation (warmth) to a visual image. It's important to note that these devices can't see or record non-solid objects such as smoke, mist, or vapors. Another thing to keep in mind is that the thermal imager can pick up heat reflected off surfaces such as mirrors, or radiating from windows, walls, even seat cushions. These false positives can result in incorrect claims of evidence for paranormal activity.

The lingering heat of a warm hand on a cold seat.

The thermal imaging device is still a valuable tool in any investigation when used correctly. In some cases, the device can pick up heat signatures of animals within the walls of a home that might be causing sounds that are being confused as paranormal activity, or it can be used to see drafts coming into an establishment that might be causing cold spots. Make sure to spend plenty of time researching the right device for your group.

In this section, we have provided the pros and cons of some of the most popular paranormal investigating devices sold on the market today. It's very important to remember that all devices are not created equal, with some of these items based on some pretty sketchy theories. It's also important to know your equipment, inside and out. This includes knowing each device's strengths, weaknesses, and limitations. Hopefully you will keep this information in mind when you see the latest flashy devices being endorsed on television or the Internet as "proven" tools for paranormal investigating.

5

Houses of Horror

From sites of unspeakable acts of cruelty, murder and mayhem, to abandoned institutions where barbaric protocols led to our modern understanding of treatment for the mentally ill, the term "house of horror" is as deceptively vague and succinctly terrible as our imaginations will allow. The locations investigated in this chapter are darker in character, and in some cases, far more sinister in nature than earlier investigations at locations I now consider far more benign.

Thornhaven Manor

About a month after our Gettysburg adventure, I received an email from John informing me that he had obtained a series of open dates to conduct an investigation at Thornhaven Manor, a nineteenth-century farmhouse in eastern Indiana. It was a little-known location that had just recently become available for paranormal investigating. The house had a rich historical context and was also the documented location of a murder. I was eager to expand my list of investigating experiences, and in short order we coordinated and reserved a date and time. Like the Gettysburg adventure, this would prove to be a lengthy haul, taking me from the northeast corner of Ohio to the far eastern fringe of central Indiana—a one-way trip of over five hundred miles.

Thankfully, a reasonable amount of documentation was available for the property, some of which makes this location legendary . . . at least in east-central Indiana. This saved us a lot of time and legwork. It's worth noting that the name "Thornhaven" is not original to the property; the current owner gave it the name because of the thorn trees that surround it.

Thornhaven was originally a farmhouse, built in 1845 on a sweeping one thousand-acre parcel of farmland by abolitionist (and later Union Colonel) Simon Powell. The property would remain in the Powell family for another one hundred years. Nestled between two much more recent housing developments and just across the road from farmland that was once part of the original property, Thornhaven is a hidden relic whose past is revealed to those willing to pull back the overgrowth from more than a century and a half of accumulated history.

To some, Thornhaven might be considered anything but extraordinary, particularly when compared to other domiciles that have survived more than 160 years of Midwestern sun, snow, and freezing temperatures. Having remained within the Powell family for a century, there's little doubt the home has witnessed its share of hardships and tragedies. There's the tragic death of Powell's youngest daughter, Lizzie, who passed away in 1853 at the age of two—and later, the death of married daughter Ester Catherine, who passed away in the home in 1875.

That said, it is not all that unusual for a person to die at home even now, and in the nineteenth century, it was much more common. But Thornhaven's past includes a historical punctuation mark that makes it unique among its contemporaries, and explains why paranormal investigators are willing to travel hundreds of miles and challenge themselves to obtain paranormal evidence in this classic haunted house.

In 1906, tenant farmer Reuben Bailey was murdered in the house by his son-in-law, Frank Thurman. Based on newspaper reports and a later jailhouse confession, Thurman ultimately confessed to raping and impregnating his younger sister-in-law, Malita Bailey. Rather than face the music of the assault and resulting pregnancy, Thurman instead decided to eliminate the entire family . . . by filling the sugar bowl with rat poison. As detailed in the newspaper articles, Reuben Bailey quickly and painfully succumbed to the toxin.

Miss Malita Bailey, a daughter of the dead man and a sister-in-law of Thurman, admitted that she was in a delicate condition and that Thurman was the author of her shame. She made an affidavit in which she charged that Thurman had criminally assaulted her. She furnished what the authorities believed to be a motive for the attempt to poison the family. It is believed that in order to prevent exposure, Thurman attempted to poison Miss Bailey and was careless as to whom else fell victims of his plans. Mrs. Bailey, Miss Bailey and Mr. Bailey were all violently ill, but Mr. Bailey was the only one whose illness proved fatal. In her affidavit Miss Bailey charged Thurman not only with assaulting her, but with causing the death of her father. Thurman was arrested and placed in jail, where it is alleged he made statements practically admitting his guilt in both offenses.

Thurman was convicted of the crime, and after numerous appeals—including one to the US Supreme Court—his life sentence was sustained. How he escaped the hangman's noose remains a mystery to me.

THIS IS A TRUE AND ACCURATE COPY OF A DOCUMENT ON FILE WITH THE INDIANA STATE ARCHIVES INDIANA COMMISSION ON PUBLIC RECORDS 6440 E. 30TH STREET INDIANAPOLIS, IN 46219

THIS IS A TRUE AND ACCURATE COPY OF A DOCUMENT ON FILE WITH THE INDIANA STATE ARCHIVES INDIANA COMMISSION ON PUBLIC RECORDS 6440 E. 30TH STREET INDIANAPOLIS, IN 46219

ROUGH ON RATS

TRADE MARK

DON'T DIE IN THE HOUSE

at that time was bordering on "tremens." He asked one of the officers to go to their house, saying there were a lot of "niggers" there raising trouble, and he couldn't get them out.

The lesson of these two deaths should impress the thoughtful, sober-minded citizenship of this community with the imperative duty of making an immediate effort to stop the traffic that blights so many lives, saddens homes, endangers the peace and safety of society, and brings untimely death.

King Alec Indicted.

Deputy Sheriff Ira Burr went to Knightstown Monday and placed Alec McCarty under arrest. The grand jury returned four indictments against McCarty for violating the Sunday closing law. McCarty gave bond in the sum of $300.

Thurman Will Stay In.

The Supreme Court has affirmed the life sentence imposed on Frank Thurman by the Henry circuit court, convicted of murdering his father-in-law, Reuben Baily, by poison, almost two years ago. It will be remembered that "Rough on Rats" was placed in the coffee.

After his arrest Thurman made complete confession of the crime, both orally, and in a signed statement. His attorneys sought to reverse the case on the ground that Thurman made confession under "duress." The people of Henry county were "with the jury" in their verdict, only that a small number thought that the death penalty should have been imposed; and so thought two members of the jury.

(How macabre that the newspaper publishers would place this ad above an update on the Thurman case!)

After several hours of driving Ohio's monotonous and construction-ridden interstates, we finally began to break free of the Buckeye State's population centers, finding ourselves on one of the Midwest's major east-west corridors and the fringe of the nation's breadbasket. New Castle, Indiana, came up quickly, and not long after finally extricating ourselves from I-70, we found ourselves at the gravel drive leading up to Thornhaven Manor.

One hundred feet from the road, beyond the chained-off driveway with the NO TRESPASSING signs, rests the faded and exhausted nineteenth-century Italianate homestead. Obscured by overgrown roses, bramble, and annuals, Thornhaven is everything you imagine when you think "haunted house." Simply awesome! Sadly, though, the manor is in rough shape. Like so many of these historic American dwellings, 160 years of hard time and brutal Midwestern weather have taken a toll.

Steven Miller, owner and proprietor of Thornhaven Manor, warmly greeted us at his relatively recent historical acquisition.

As a lifelong resident of the area, Steve explained that he had always had a love for the house and its rich past, and when it went up for auction, he jumped at the opportunity—though he confessed he didn't realize he would end up in a bidding war with a developer who would have unceremoniously demolished the structure to build new homes. "I wasn't going to let that happen," Steve remarked.

Steve is a great guy, and I give him and all who devote themselves to this type of historic preservation immense thanks, respect, and appreciation for their efforts and fortitude. I say this with all sincerity, because when we were given our tour of Thornhaven, I was shocked at the condition of the interior. The general structure (siding, walls, floors, windows) and the foundation were mostly intact, but time, disrepair, and decay had taken a serious toll on the manor.

While the front living room and adjacent parlor were solid and dry, the rear portion of the first floor (kitchen and formal dining room) were in rough shape. Actually, calling it *rough* would be a polite understatement. In the rear corner of the kitchen, the walls had separated from the ceiling, creating a large, gash-like void, fully exposing the kitchen to wind and weather; the corner had been cordoned off. Worse still was the dining room: At the time of our investigation, the floor was literally gone, having collapsed into the basement. That area was also cordoned off. The second floor was in far better structural condition, with all floors, walls, and ceilings joined. Although the fireplaces on both floors were also intact, we found a lot of dust, mortar, and debris in all the grates, suggesting that the chimneys were crumbling.

This would truly be an adventure and a challenge! Adding to all this was the fact that electrical service had not yet been restored . . . for good reason. I'm certain the slightest fault would have set the whole house ablaze. In preparation for this new challenge, we came prepared with heavy-duty portable battery power that would operate the DVR systems though we had no idea for how long. It was a crapshoot; we would get as much

DVR recording time as the battery provided and rely most heavily on the portable night-vision camcorders.

As daylight began to fade to dusk, we hustled with the setup. By this time I had become quite good at it and needed very little direction. While John pulled and wired up the monitor and console in the living room, I set and wired the DVR cameras and placed audio recorders throughout the house. As we conducted the setup, late-day sunlight from the front of the house mixed with the eerie, musty darkness that was accumulating in the rear, creating a creepy gloom that played on the senses and accentuated the "vibe" I have spoken of previously. This was the most dilapidated structure I had ever set foot in, and though I had already trampled through the accessible portions of the house, setting cameras and laying cable, I couldn't shake what seemed like a different creep factor, one I had never before experienced.

As I reflect on the experience, I realize it was akin to weary defensiveness, perhaps even agitation. This place was dangerous, and if we were not careful, someone could get seriously injured. Though dark, romantic images of *The Fall of the House of Usher* may have tickled my imagination, along with any of Thornhaven's resident ghosts, horror movie images also plagued me—especially the trope of the guy falling through the floor and getting impaled on God knows what in the black hole below. What I really needed was a strong dose of coffee and some fresh air. So while John completed the setup, I took a dash around the block to a nearby Quickie Mart to load up on caffeine and snacks.

I will take this opportunity to make yet another personal confession: I have always been leery of wearing my C-Bus T-shirt in public. Though I'm certainly not embarrassed of what I'm doing or the company I keep, especially during an investigation, prominently displaying the term *paranormal* across my chest (tantamount to a billboard) has always made me uneasy about the unsolicited comments, inquiries, and conversations that such advertisements might provoke. I mention this at this point because when I entered the Quickie Mart, the cashier and his associate made enthusiastic inquiries and engaged me in a conversation about the paranormal. After informing them of our investigation at Thornhaven—which was familiar to both of them—they told me about their belief that a ghost resided there at the Quickie Mart. They went on to describe several incidents they believed were attributed to a ghostly presence.

Though I felt like replying, "Dude, I just want some coffee," I patiently listened and answered their general questions as best I could. Truth is, I'm a very approachable guy (modest, too). However, when it comes to the subject of paranormal phenomena, I tend to be a little reserved. It has been my experience that people's responses and reactions to and about the subject run the complete spectrum, from complete deniers who simply guffaw, to spiritual and religious folks who have their own strong opinions or beliefs regarding the nature and cause of the phenomena and whether people should be engaged in such investigating activities at all. Then there are the folks— as I observed at the tanning salon—who can become anxious, distressed, or even horrified at the idea. Since I don't always know whom I'm speaking with or their perspective, opinions, and beliefs, I tend to avoid these types of discussions.

Simply put, I am *not* trying to prove anything to anyone . . . other than myself. Investigating paranormal phenomena is an existential experience, and though I work hard to maintain my objectivity, I always come back to the reality that *all* of this stuff is experimental, and there are neither experts in this field, nor black-and-white truths or answers . . . at least not yet. I must also emphasize that my personal foibles, like worrying about wearing the shirt in public, reflect my own insecurities. The reality is that at worst the shirt has elicited strange looks, and at best I have received the occasional thumbs-up and subtle *I like your shirt* remarks or simple friendly inquiries like *Are you a ghost hunter?*

Extricating myself from the Quickie Mart, I returned to Thornhaven, which was slipping from shadowy gloom into complete darkness—and (as John explained) was beginning to come alive in its own subtle way with little taps and knocks. Like all our investigations, Thornhaven comprised a series of walk-throughs. Generally, the initial sweep tends to consist of short stays in each of the rooms. Though we are always on the lookout (and listen-out) for visual and audio phenomena, we are also establishing a baseline. Haunted or not, buildings, like people, have their own unique fingerprints relative to light and sound. We need to know how a room captures and reflects natural sunlight, moonlight, daytime heating and nighttime cooling, and how these might interact with or affect our infrared equipment.

We carefully listen to and try to isolate the location of sounds, like those taps and knocks I mentioned earlier. There are usually logical and commonsense explanations for the sounds often heard in a house (haunted or not), regardless of its condition. Of course, factors such as condition of repair and whether there is water and/or electric service play a major factor in trying to determine the cause or source of sights and sounds. The fact that Thornhaven had neither water nor electric service actually helped us to determine whether the sounds we were hearing were natural or unusual.

On the flipside, Thornhaven's decrepit state made our attempts at distinguishing the more unusual sounds and noises from those natural for Thornhaven a lot harder. Here lies the difference between an investigator and a thrill-seeker: thrill-seekers tend to label all the sights and sounds as paranormal; real investigators are much more reserved in their determinations. Needless to say, that doesn't mean that we don't sometimes have the crap scared out of us by completely natural occurrences.

Case in point: while conducting one of our many EVP sessions on the second floor of Thornhaven, we began hearing sounds from the kitchen area beneath us. We quickly descended the stairs and entered the kitchen, where we continued our recording. That's when the growling began ... then a sudden mad dash scratching and scrambling from inside the wall immediately next to us. Startling? Absolutely! Paranormal? Hardly. Clearly, some varmint (raccoon, squirrel, who knows?) had taken up residence inside the wall.

For a couple more hours, we continued our slow, methodical progress throughout the house. We were then joined, rather unexpectedly, by Wendy Jessie and Anissa Marsh, two members of New Castle's own Girls of the Dark paranormal team, both friends of Thornhaven and Steve's resident paranormal team. After exchanging pleasantries, Wendy, Anissa, and Steve joined us in a series of EVP sessions throughout the house. It's interesting to note, particularly after completing our audio review for evidence, that the few bits of evidence we did obtain directly correspond to the period of time they were with us. This lends credence to the belief that spirits can react quite differently based on the gender and/or familiarity of the people investigating.

When you think about it, it makes perfect sense. Spirits (just like people) can behave differently in the company of people they feel an association or connection with, such as at Thornhaven, or in an environment where the absence of women might stir feelings of longing, regret, resentment—or other, more carnal desires—as at the Ohio State Reformatory in Mansfield, where the inmate population was 100 percent male.

After the ladies departed, the energy in the house changed. Though we continued the investigation for a few more hours, we concluded that whoever still resides in Thornhaven, be it the maternal Ester Catherine, the unfortunate Reuben Bailey, or little Lizzie Powell, had already said their piece for the night or had no interest in interacting with a couple of guys. Regardless, it was clear that we'd gotten what we were going to get, and the investigation was over.

Here are the bits of evidence we collected at Thornhaven Manor.

bit.ly/ghostlyencounters-thornhaven

Our next series of investigations would take us deep into the heart of America's breadbasket: rural Iowa, where we would explore two distinctly different sites over a long weekend. Our first stop was Scotch Grove, Iowa. This was the home of Edinburgh Manor, originally constructed as a county poor farm, then converted into a regional asylum and finally repurposed as a retirement home that was closed in 2010. The second location and highlight of our trip, roughly three hundred miles southeast of Edinburgh, is perhaps one of America's most infamous and iconic haunted locations: the Villisca Axe Murder House, where on a warm June night in 1912 an entire family was savagely murdered in their sleep.

I can tell you that the ten-hour drive from Ohio to Iowa was unlike any of the other road trips we had taken. Certainly the distance was noteworthy but so too was the mood . . . an eerie mix of exhilaration and fearful trepidation. There was an unmistakable pall that permeated our usual excitement. Though we had been to some sad and equally freaky locations, the Villisca house was a historic site unlike anything either one of us had experienced. Of course, we were excited and looking forward to finally *doing* the Villisca house, but we were also keenly aware that the site, an otherwise ordinary house in rural America, was a place where a singular horrific and gruesome event has forever stained the house, the town, and the historic record with the blood of innocents—a true American hell-house.

For all intents and purposes, we would be spending the night at an unsolved crime scene, one that continues to baffle investigators and historians. It was that knowledge that placed the gloom in both our minds. However, we will get to Villisca a little later. Our first night would be spent investigating the little-known Edinburgh Manor.

Edinburgh Manor

In 1846, the land where Edinburgh now stands was first granted by county officials for the establishment of a county poor farm. The farm would also house the disabled and incurably insane. According to Edinburgh's site administrator, Edinburgh, formerly the Jones County Poor Farm, was originally a pair of residential farmhouses where able-bodied tenants raised crops and livestock. In the *History of Jones County, Iowa, Past and Present,* published in 1910, the poor farm was described as:

General farming is practiced. The beneficiaries of the institution average fully twenty in constant attendance, and comprise nearly all nationalities and all colors, and all ages, from the nursling to the veteran of nearly ninety winters. The county is burdened with several who are incurably insane. While the policy of the county is to decline furnishing a comfortable retreat for all the lazy, able-bodied, willingly dependent applicants for its charities, nevertheless, the treatment of all its unfortunates is considerate and humane[6].

---

[6]   R. M. Corbitt, *History of Jones County, Iowa, Past and Present;* (Chicago: S. J. Clarke Publishing Co., 1910)

During its sixty years as a functioning poor farm, there were more than eighty documented deaths; most of those who died are buried in the adjacent cemetery. In 1910, the poor farm was closed and dismantled, making room for the construction of a new, more modern facility that was completed in 1911. Its purpose, generally unchanged, was to house the incurably insane, the poor, and the elderly. Edinburgh Manor would operate for another ninety-nine years before closing its doors for good in 2010.

After nearly ten hours of driving, it was good to finally arrive somewhere, even if that somewhere was the middle of nowhere ... and Scotch Grove truly *is* in the middle of nowhere. With the day shot and the sun beginning to set, we had no idea what technical challenges would confront us. Similar in size, scope, and appearance to the Madison Seminary, the building was composed of two primary wings where patients or residents were divided by gender; women were housed in the left wing, men on the right. Based on appearances, we expected the entire facility to be in a condition similar to its outward appearance ... generally good. This would prove to be a mistaken assumption.

When we arrived, we were warmly greeted by Edinburgh's Administrator and Tour Coordinator (who asked not to be mentioned by name in this text), who proceeded to give us a quick tour of the facility. Though highly knowledgeable of the Manor's history, she also made it abundantly clear at the onset that she really didn't like being in the building after dark. We respected her discomfort and kept the chit chat to a minimum, allowing her to conduct the walk-through at her pace. Normally, in buildings of similar size, such as Madison, the initial walk-through can take anywhere from forty-five minutes to an hour. The administrator completed her tour in twenty minutes. Ten minutes after that, she was in her car headed down the gravel drive, leaving us to lock up when we were finished. It wasn't until later that we came to fully appreciate her discomfort.

As I mentioned, Edinburgh's outward appearance was deceiving, and though the bones and general structure were in generally good shape, as were many of the rooms and common areas, several areas of the main level and most of the basement were significantly water damaged and stained. A major freeze a few years before had caused several pipes to burst, causing substantial damage that was ultimately too costly to repair. Subsequently, water service to the building was cut off and the mess was cleaned up as best as possible. As the following pictures clearly indicate, after a plumbing catastrophe, the resulting moisture damage creates its own nightmare over time.

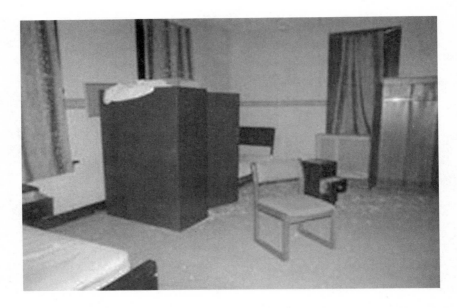

With night quickly descending, we decided to scrap the DVR and limit the video to the mobile night-vision camcorders. As John began pulling equipment, I stepped out into the cold night to have a smoke before "round one." It was then that I saw the proverbial wall closing in on me; I was exhausted—we were both exhausted—and though we were truly pumped about finally getting started, something just didn't feel right. That's when John came out and said, "We need to get started—this place is coming alive. I'm hearing banging and heavy footsteps up on two."

The adrenalin surged and I felt my second wind kick in. Upon re-entering the building, there was a definite palpable vibe, very intense and not very welcoming. We quickly geared up and got under way.

This was truly a weird investigation. Unlike other locations, we soon began discovering strange bits of physical evidence, artifacts if you will, scattered throughout the residents' rooms and common areas. Some of these artifacts were both sad and even a little disturbing—dare I say *haunting*.

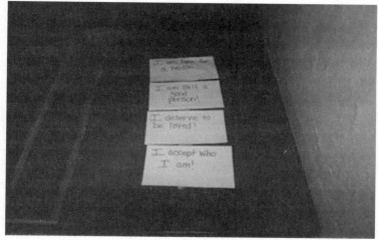

In the basement laundry, haphazard heaps of clothing and nightgowns had been left behind, wispy remnants of the former residents . . . as if waiting to be reclaimed.

Of course, we conducted numerous EVP sessions, sometimes hearing answering knocks and taps, other times not. In one session on the second-floor foyer that separated the men's and women's rooms, an area the administrator pointed out as being highly active, we heard (and recorded) the following disembodied voice.

bit.ly/ghostlyencounters-edinburgh

As the hours quickly passed, the vibe and the noises that were apparent earlier began to wane. We were also exhausted, and mutually agreed that we were finished. After six hours of Edinburgh Manor, we wrapped up the investigation, packed it in, and headed off to a hotel. These are the bits of paranormal evidence we obtained from Edinburgh Manor.

bit.ly/ghostlyencounters-edinburgh

By 4:00 a.m., we had unpacked the car of all our equipment and were in our meager accommodations. By 4:05 a.m., we were both fast asleep and didn't stir for ten hours.

There's no disputing that the road trip to Iowa kicked both our butts. Of course, investigating Edinburgh Manor also destroyed us physically. Truth is, spending six hours in Edinburgh was much more of a health risk than I'd ever imagined. With so much water damage throughout the building, I'm certain the air we were breathing was nothing less than a toxic soup of mold and bacteria that in actuality made us both sick. Thankfully, we purposely built in an extra day for rest and recuperation before our appointment with the Villisca house. When we finally awoke, we ate like horses and returned to the hotel, where we dozed through a *Lost In Space* marathon and slept for another ten hours.

Why have I included Edinburgh Manor in a chapter entitled *Houses of Horror*? With eighty confirmed deaths and one known suicide during its life as a functioning institution, we should not be fooled into thinking an old country home in a pastoral setting was anything less than a warehouse for the aged and infirm. Of course, all things are relative; compared with the other locations presented in this chapter, Edinburgh was an idyllic paradise. Edinburgh also taught us a valuable procedural lesson: the musty smell of damp and decay is a red flag to be wary of the air you're breathing, and if necessary, to protect yourself. Upon our return from Iowa, we immediately added respirators to our kits.

The Villisca Axe Murder House

Author's Note: The Villisca Axe Murders case is, in many ways, a seductive path that leads you into a bizarre place of limited facts, strange details, and even more unanswered questions. Several quality books and a few DVDs have tried to piece together the historical information in an attempt to make sense of these senseless crimes. However, as a writer, I now find myself stepping very gingerly onto the trailhead of the story. . . because it is easy, too easy, to be drawn in, wanting to know more. I will tread this path only lightly and briefly, and leave it to you, the reader, to follow your own curiosity and desire to learn more.

After a four-hour car ride out of Cedar Rapids, through a sea of cornfields and wind farms, we were at last at our destination: the worn and weathered town of Villisca, Iowa. The day was gray, cold and damp—fitting weather it seemed, for an investigation at this infamous paranormal house of horror. There is indeed a veil of gloom and sadness that overtakes you when you step onto the property and look for the first time at this nondescript, unimpressive little house, particularly on a dreary autumn day. Since the horrendous and tragic events more than a century ago, the stain of death still hangs heavy on the place.

In my opinion, no honest, life-loving person who knows what happened here can look upon this place and not be moved. To me, the irony of the Villisca house is that it is so small and plain—what you and I would think of as a starter home for a newlywed couple or young family. And in that context, that small reflective connection, the real horrors unfold.

These are the facts: On the evening of June 9, 1912, Mr. Josiah Moore (a prominent local businessman) and his family, along with sleepover guests, Lena and Ina Stillinger (friends of daughter Katherine), returned home from a children's pageant at the nearby Presbyterian church. The church social concluded at 9:30 p.m., with the family and their guests returning to the house somewhere between 9:45 and 10:00 p.m. It was the last time they were seen alive.

By 7:00 a.m., next-door-neighbor Mary Peckham felt something was wrong. The daily chores at the Moore house had not been started, and the normally active child-filled house was uncharacteristically silent. Upon investigation, she found the house was locked (unusual at the time), and after several unanswered knocks, she immediately called Josiah's brother, Ross Moore. Ross quickly called the drugstore Josiah managed; he was not there and had not been seen. He then hurried to the house.

When he arrived, both Ross and Mary circled the house, attempting to peer into and even rap on the curtain-drawn windows. There was no reply, not a sound.

Nervously, Ross used his spare key and unlocked the home, tentatively entering the front parlor. Mary remained on the porch. Nothing appeared out of place and all was still, not a sound disturbing the silence. Ross called his brother's name, then Sarah's; there was no reply. Stepping to the doorway of the first-floor bedroom, his eyes fell upon blood-spattered walls and blood-soaked bedding. Panic-stricken, he bolted from the scene, frantically shouting at Mary to call the sheriff.

All eight people in the house were dead . . . their heads bludgeoned and hacked far beyond recognition, Josiah worst of them all. A bloodstained axe was found nearby.

The victims of the Villisca massacre included:

Mr. Josiah B. Moore; father, age 43

Mrs. Sarah Moore; mother, age 39

Herman Moore; son, age 11

Katherine Moore; daughter, age 9

Boyd Moore; son, age 7

Paul Moore; son, age 5

Lena Stillinger; friend, age 12

Ina Stillinger; friend, age 7

To describe the massacre as savage and vicious would be an understatement. Eyewitness accounts suggest that each of the victims received no less than thirty strikes each; however, modern investigators discount the claims as exaggerations, explaining that so many blows would have reduced the skulls to piles of fragments. Of course, that does not lessen the brutality: all of their heads had been horrifically battered and smashed— six children, two adults.

In the hours that followed, while calls for additional law enforcement were made and the coroner and local doctors summoned, the stunned and curious began to assemble. Some even entered the premises, wanting to see the horror for themselves, with items and mementos taken as souvenirs. By late afternoon, the National Guard arrived and effectively secured the house, but it was too late. The damage had been done, the crime scene completely compromised.

With virtually no physical evidence other than the murder weapon, detectives and law enforcement officials made every possible attempt at finding and capturing the fugitive murderer(s). Bloodhounds were brought to the scene, searches conducted, trails and other possible escape routes plotted and followed, transients and vagrants apprehended. All leads were followed, but to no avail.

In the weeks and months that followed, the real detective work began. With literally no useful physical evidence, Sheriff Oren Jackson and Federal Agent M. W. McClaughry began exploring motive in the hopes of uncovering suspects. Of the eight victims, Josiah was by far the most brutally ravaged, suggesting the murders might have been a revenge or vendetta killing.

Exploring Josiah's past revealed some interesting clues. This led detectives to suspect the possible involvement of Frank Jones, a well-known local politician who had served in the House of Representatives and state senate. Jones was also a wealthy businessman who had previously employed Josiah Moore in his general merchandise business. After several years of employment, the two apparently had a bitter falling-out that led to Josiah Moore quitting his job and beginning a competing general merchandise business of his own. The rivalry would become toxic when Frank Jones eventually lost the exclusive and highly lucrative John Deere plow contract to Josiah Moore's new business venture. If that wasn't enough, rumors swirled through town that Josiah had had an affair with Frank Jones's daughter-in-law.

Of course, axe murdering is a messy business, not the kind of work for respectable businessmen and politicians. However, respectable businessmen and politicians have the ways and means to employ others to do their dirty work—someone like a deranged vagrant, one William Mansfield. Though the theory was both plausible and convenient to some, lack of evidence and a corroborated alibi would ultimately eliminate Mansfield as a viable suspect.

The most likely of suspects came in the form of a diminutive preacher from nearby Macedonia, Iowa—the Reverend George Kelly, who was in Villisca at the time of the murders. Described as scrawny, excitable, and not very fond of children, Kelly had been present at the children's program at the Presbyterian Church and had departed town at approximately the same time the bodies were discovered.

Rumors abounded regarding Kelly and his strange behavior. It was believed that he had sent a bloody shirt to be laundered that night, but no such evidence was ever found. It was rumored he had been heard muttering "Slay, and slay utterly," the night of the murders, but this too had never been substantiated. Perhaps the most damning circumstantial evidence came during his scheduled train ride out of Villisca, where he was heard discussing the murders hours before the discovery. Then, in 1917, while still under investigation for the murders, Kelly confessed . . . only to recant the confession at trial. Ultimately, he was acquitted for lack of evidence.

The Villisca Axe Murders remains one of the saddest unsolved murder mysteries in American history, and though all we can do is nod our heads in morose bewilderment, we can't lose sight of the fact that these grisly crimes occurred during a truly bygone era, when the absence of knowledge, science, and technology worked to a killer's advantage. In the decade that followed, quantum leaps in the advancement of investigation and analysis would likewise bring a revolution in criminology that would directly impact everyone and everything, from the federal level all the way down to the local level.

Though horrendous crimes still occur every day, there is solace in knowing that society has in fact learned lessons from the past, and even though there are still unsolved crimes that plague law enforcement, a repeat of the Villisca slaughter is unlikely to happen again. I can't help but wonder if somewhere, buried deep in some forgotten trunk or footlocker, some key piece of evidence is waiting to be revealed.

After paying our respects to the Moore and Stillinger families at the Villisca Cemetery, we went to the house, set up all of our equipment, and got the investigation under way. Oddly enough, unlike many other locations we have investigated, the Villisca house lacked that uncomfortable vibe and feeling that you're not alone or that you're being watched.

Since the house is in fact quite small, we were set and recording in about thirty minutes, effectively covering each of the three bedrooms, the attic, the parlor, and the kitchen area. For the next eight hours we respectfully attempted to interact and communicate with any of the house's lingering spirits. This included simply asking questions, reading stories, and engaging in child's play.

As is so often the case, we found the house to be very quiet throughout the investigation. There were no apparitions or shadow people, no disembodied voices such as the female we had heard two nights earlier at Edinburgh. Though we had certainly hoped to observe and document dramatic paranormal activity, like slamming doors or voices intelligently answering our questions, we both knew you can't judge the level of activity until you have patiently and deliberately reviewed all of the raw audio and video. Thus, after a lengthy and thorough investigation of the Villisca Axe Murder House, we pulled our sleeping bags from the car, let the audio and video equipment run . . . and caught a few hours of sleep on the living room floor . . . strange, to have slept so soundly under the same roof and mere feet away from such a horrendous death scene.

Though the Villisca house did not deliver the dramatic experience that makes for good reality television, Villisca did not disappoint. Here is the evidence we obtained:

bit.ly/ghostlyencounters-villisca

Based on this evidence and the evidence of other investigative teams who have posted their evidence in the public domain, it is obvious that several spirits inhabit the house. The voices of children are the most common, but there is also the voice or voices of one, possibly more, adult males who decidedly don't like children. This has led some to speculate that the spirit of the Villisca axe killer also resides in the house.

Although the supposition is tantalizing, I think it's a stretch. I tend to believe that the presence of child spirits in the house has attracted other more localized spirits—perhaps a crabby, mean-spirited old-timer who likes the energy and attention but really dislikes everything else, particularly the children. (We all know the type.) I prefer to think that though the lost children of the Villisca nightmare do in fact frequent their death scene, they are at least free of the monster that brutally ended their lives. Of course, that is complete conjecture on my part.

While we are on the subject of the negative or malevolent spirit believed to be attached to the Villisca house, I am compelled to add a brief footnote and heartfelt investigative confession: on one of the famous ghost shows, a paranormal celeb brought an axe into the house, hoping to provoke the malevolent spirit and stir up some excitement. In my opinion, anyone who would bring an axe into the Villisca house to use as a *trigger object* needs to have his or her own head examined . . . professionally.

Though the theory and practice of using *trigger objects* or *devices* to promote or enhance paranormal phenomena has an absolutely appropriate place in the wider discussion of investigating methods, I strongly believe the decision to employ the strategy and the specific object(s) used must likewise be thoughtfully squared in ethics and simple common sense . . . regardless of the television production value. My god, six children and two adults had their heads smashed to bits in the house—show a little respect! In my opinion, the people who make and support these types of choices are not investigators, they are ghouls. *(Sigh.)*

With the summer coming to an end, the 2013 investigating season was also winding down. The wrap of the season and the calendar year would bring some big changes for me. Having recently sent my son off to college in Cincinnati, I found myself an empty nester and at a bit of a crossroads personally and professionally. I truly loved small-town living and the school community that had embraced me, but life on Lake Erie's coast had taken its toll on me physically. Though I often quipped that even as the oldest member of the C-Bus team, I could still run circles around most of my younger colleagues, I found the Cleveland winters becoming colder and snowier, my house getting bigger and bigger, and the maintenance less and less fun. I was ready for a change, and with a large chunk of my family down south in Atlanta, a much more agreeable climate, relocation was a no-brainer. Still, C-Bus Paranormal had a busy schedule, particularly with Halloween right around the corner.

Perhaps one of the team's most fun and exciting opportunities came when C-Bus Paranormal hosted two public Halloween Ghost Hunts at the place where it all started for me, the Madison Seminary. Since those earliest investigations, I had always wanted to organize and conduct a *hunt* at the seminary—to provide small teams and curious enthusiasts an opportunity to see what an investigation was all about, where . . . quite possibly . . . a person might be able to have their own paranormal experience. Learning and teaching seems as much a part of me as my glasses and beard.

With careful planning that began eight months earlier, we welcomed individuals from Pennsylvania, Indiana, and as far away as New Mexico, as well as enthusiasts and small teams from throughout Ohio. In an effort to preserve a relatively quiet atmosphere for people to record their own EVP sessions, we purposely capped each night at a maximum of twenty-five participants. Both nights quickly sold out, and the feedback was extremely positive.

Though we set up the DVR system and ran audio for both events, primarily to exhibit the equipment and its uses, the few tantalizing audio hits we obtained have never been included on the team's evidence page. It was unanimously agreed that since there were upwards of thirty people walking and talking throughout the buildings, any potential evidence would be suspect. I did, however, manage to capture a tidbit that I'm happy to share with you. The audio you are about to hear was obtained on the second night. As the owner was finishing her tour with the participants, I ducked out with my recorder and went up to the third-floor hallway, the same location where Andrew had been decked during our first visit.

In the time since that first investigation at Madison Seminary, I had come to realize that the entity I had previously characterized as a belligerent nurse maybe wasn't so belligerent after all. Maybe she was being protective of her wards; maybe she didn't like a bunch of people invading her space and then questioning her existence. Maybe she was just tired of hearing the same old questions and requests, over and over again, like, "Can you give us a sign of your presence?" Perhaps our earlier experiences were more of a reflection of our beliefs, influences, and preconceived notions rather than the actual natures of the entities that inhabit the seminary.

Perhaps it's the lifelong learner in me that seeks to reflect and improve, whether teaching a classroom of seventh graders or attempting to communicate with the ghost of an early twentieth-century psychiatric nurse. To me it's about upping my game, so with recorder in hand, I went to the third-floor corridor and tried having a casual conversation with someone I was beginning to feel was more of an acquaintance than an amorphous energy anomaly. To me, the experience was . . . enlightening.

bit.ly/ghostlyencounters-madison2

As the nostalgic old-fogey of the group, I find it fitting and proper that my last investigation for the year was at Madison. A week later, I put my house on the market, loaded up the truck, and moved to Atlanta.

The Bell Nursing Home

With family close by and career opportunities aplenty, Atlanta proved to be a wise move. Though the city was paralyzed by the famous "Snowpocalypse" not long after my arrival, Atlanta's winter was much more agreeable and much less painful. Of course, I was also looking forward to the spring of 2014 and the start-up of the investigating season. John and I had finally inked the deal for this book, yet felt we needed to include a few more locations.

With me in Atlanta and the rest of the team in Ohio, careful coordination of schedules and locations would be critical. For us, that meant a series of doubleheaders: two investigations over the span of a weekend. To be honest, doubleheaders suck—big-time. As the Iowa trip had taught us, great distances coupled with tight schedules make for a less than ideal investigating mind-set. However, we now had a book deal and associated deadline. We're both also gainfully employed and didn't have the luxury of committing several weekends over the period of a summer. We'd simply have to suck it up. Thus, on the first weekend of June 2014, I loaded up the Buick and headed back north. Our first destination was Kimbolton, Ohio, where we would first investigate the Bell Nursing Home. The following night, we would hustle south to Radford, Virginia, and St. Albans Sanatorium.

Approximately twenty miles north of the junction of Interstates 77 and 70 in southeastern Ohio is the small town of Kimbolton, population 144. Like Scotch Grove and Villisca, Kimbolton is in the middle of Nowhere, Ohio—which of course adds its own mysterious and creepy dimension to an investigation. This one would be a little different from our previous C-Bus Paranormal investigations in that we were partnering with a small Youngstown, Ohio-based team we had met at the Madison Seminary public hunts: Ohio Lost Souls Paranormal, founded by Christopher Oles.

I had the opportunity of getting to know Chris via Craigslist, where I had been trying to sell an infrared illuminator. In the months that followed Chris's initial inquiry into my Phantom Lite and the ensuing correspondence, we had established an appreciation for the way our teams conduct investigations and the disdain we both had for a lot of the crap that was being produced for paranormal reality television. Chris is also a licensed electrician, whose obvious professional expertise brings great value to investigating and the interpretation of evidence obtained.

Much like television's paranormal plumbers, experience in any of the trades, particularly electrical and plumbing, goes a long way toward understanding and explaining (a.k.a. debunking) some of the experiences people have and some of the weird ways devices and gadgets can behave in a house or building, haunted or not.

Since the Madison ghost hunts, Chris had expressed great interest in partnering on an investigation at the Bell Nursing Home, a location not far from his home in the Youngstown area. Though I was unfamiliar with the location, Bell was a spot that was on John's bucket list, and I was certainly interested in participating, but traveling 650 miles to investigate a site that I was completely unfamiliar with and that lacked a reasonably documented past didn't seem like the best use of my time. I felt we needed to squeeze more out of a weekend devoted to investigating.

That's when I learned from Matt Slozer, an Internet friend and founder of Autumn Moon Paranormal (Winston-Salem, North Carolina), that his team would be conducting a private investigation at St. Albans Sanatorium in Radford, Virginia, that same weekend. St. Albans was a place that both John and I were definitely interested in investigating, and thankfully, Matt was open to including us in their private investigation.

Unlike public *ghost hunts* that, as the name implies, are open to all members of the public, private investigations are closed events where teams pay the admission fee and have exclusive use or access to the facility for the duration of the investigation. Since private investigations naturally limit the number of participants moving throughout a building and significantly minimize the amount of audio contamination from other participants, they are always the preferred choice, particularly for serious investigators.

Of course, the luxury of having a location to yourself and your team comes with an associated expense, oftentimes making private investigations of larger and more popular sites cost prohibitive. Our participation with Autumn Moon Paranormal would help defray their costs for exclusive access to the building. From an investigating perspective, it was a win–win for everyone involved . . . even though John and I were setting ourselves up physically for another butt whoopin'!

As noted, there's not a lot of quality source information on the Bell Nursing Home, which as a nonfiction writer makes me uncomfortable, especially when I only have "*supposed lies*" and *"rumor has it"* to go on. Though I'm hesitant to spend a great deal of time, energy, or ink on the Bell, this little-known location in an equally little-known crossroads town proved to be a real education in its own way.

Based on the sketchy information and secondary sources, this is what I've learned: The Bell Nursing Home was originally built as a residence by Andrew Ledlie in the mid-1800s, at a time when Kimbolton was a thriving small town. Located within twenty miles of Cambridge, Ohio, Kimbolton was a growing commercial railroad stop for the export of coal, timber, and other goods. The home stayed in the Ledlie family, passing from father to son William, who took over the house and family business after the passing of his father. About fifteen years later (September 1902), William passed away in the house, and the home and business were sold.

After ownership by the Ledlies, the house's chronology becomes sketchy. It's generally believed the house was first converted into a tannery and then a funeral home in the 1940s. In the 1960s, the building was purchased by Raymond Bell, who built two additions off the rear of the original structure, converting the house into a nursing home.

Sadly, not long after its opening, *rumors* emerged that the Bell Nursing Home quickly ran into trouble with local and state authorities for overcrowded and unsanitary conditions. In 2006, the Bell Nursing Home was closed, and the property essentially sat abandoned for about five years until its recent purchase by Natalie Dickendasher. With the home's close proximity to Salt Fork State Park and other public and private hunting lands, it is Natalie's hope to convert the building into a bed and breakfast.

It was during the initial cleanup and preliminary renovations of the property that Natalie realized there was more to the Bell Home than met the eye: shadows, disembodied voices, and slamming doors, just to name a few. Though certainly enticing, without much documented historical information, I was a little skeptical . . . but no less hopeful. I would certainly keep my eyes, ears, and mind open while we were there.

On the night of the investigation, both teams converged at the Bob Evans restaurant in Cambridge, Ohio. Chris's team was well represented, with a total of six teammates in attendance. Unfortunately, neither Andrew nor Julie could attend, so once again, it would just be John and me representing C–Bus Paranormal.

After a lively meal where many investigation stories and experiences were shared, we headed out of Cambridge for the quick jaunt north to Kimbolton and the Bell. There we were met by Natalie, who provided a quick tour and added a few interesting tidbits to the vague information we had collected. Apparently, Raymond Bell was a superstitious fellow who, from the onset, was uncomfortable with the house's funeral home past. In an effort to assuage his fears, he completely bricked up the embalming room—leaving equipment, devices, and God knows what else in that space. It currently remains sealed.

With the tour complete, Natalie gave us lock–up instructions and left us to our investigation. Both teams immediately got to work setting up equipment. For John and me, setup had become a well–rehearsed routine; I set up cameras and strung cable, and he set up the DVR in what was the central nursing station. While we were doing our thing, Chris's team set up six battery–powered remote IR cameras with illuminators and several digital voice recorders. Within about thirty minutes, both teams were ready to begin.

Besides bringing down costs, one of the great benefits of partnering with other investigating teams is the opportunity to see how others work together and conduct their investigations. Though it is true that everyone is looking to capture that golden paranormal moment and experience, hopefully on audio or video, the way teams go about obtaining their data is not always equal. It has been our experience that within the first twenty minutes, we know whether an investigator or team has their act together and their head(s) in the game. Still, as the invited guests of Ohio Lost Souls Paranormal, this was Chris's investigation to direct, and although he already knew our level of skill, ability, and seriousness, he was quite aware that we were now observing him and his team.

I don't want to fold any unnecessary drama into this mix because we are not investigating prima donnas. I am now, as I was back then, a student in this field, which as far as I'm concerned is both a strength and asset. I am always asking questions, *ad nauseam* to some . . . John tolerates me nonetheless. At the same time, this isn't rocket science either. Actually, it's rather instinctual: pointing cameras toward alleged hot spots and trying to capture as much as a camera lens will allow. Sure, the TV guys often give the impression of great complexity. In reality, it's not complex at all . . . or rather, it's as complex as you choose to make it.

Once we were set, Chris called a quick huddle. This was obviously not his first rodeo. Having investigated the Bell Home on three previous occasions, once as an invited guest speaker, he was the resident expert who knew this place well. He reminded us of his previous experiences and where the hot spots were. He then assigned two crew members video monitor duty; the Bell Home has a built-in video surveillance system that teams can plug into. Bell's system plus our own DVR effectively covered every square inch of the building's interior. Chris then paired his remaining team members into two smaller groups. One group he sent to the second floor of house, the second to one of the two resident wings. John and I were left to our devices, with free rein to explore wherever and however we wished.

Of course, Chris's biggest concern was to avoid walking and talking over each other. "Keep the chatter to a minimum and let's see what we can find," he advised us. The huddle broke and away we went.

It doesn't require a great deal of imagination to think of places like the Bell Home and Edinburgh Manor as occupied and fully functional institutions . . . especially since both places were fully furnished. This is where the creep factor really sets in.

Of course, a collection of freaky dolls and an old piano in the dining hall,
rumored to play on its own sometimes, doesn't help.

Geared up with our night-vision camcorders, John and I began our investigation in the second, unoccupied wing. As you can see in the photographs above, the Bell is a relatively small building with corridors not much more than two hundred feet in length with five rooms per side, making it easy for an average person to walk the full length of the corridor in fifteen to twenty seconds. Still, a building's size can be extremely deceptive as it relates to phenomena that might occur; there's simply no consistency. Sometimes spirit activity can be concentrated or focused in a single area, other times not. It seems the nature of paranormal phenomenon directly corresponds with the nature of the entity or entities that are producing it. In spite of the building's size, we quickly focused our attention to both the *vibe* and the quiet that surrounded us. Like so many places we have been, there was the uncanny sense of being watched by unfriendly eyes. Then there are the sounds a building makes, some more obvious than others—like the drip of faucet or the wind through an old, unsealed window.

Of the haunted locations we have visited, I often felt that some ghosts, like people, would toy with us, making innocuous noises such as subtle taps on a window or knocks on a door. Hell, if I were a ghost, I'd probably do the same thing. Oftentimes, investigators—ourselves included—will ask a spirit to respond to a question with a knock or series of knocks. Perhaps the most familiar and frequently used knocking/tapping strategy is the "shave and a haircut ... two bits" sequence (tap–tap–tap–tap–tap ... tap–tap), where the investigator will ask the ghost to reply to the first part of the sequence with the final two taps. Though it may seem kind of dumb, getting an entity to reply in rhythm, time, and sequence is by all means very encouraging. Getting an entity to tap out the reply several times is typically viewed as strong evidence of a paranormal interaction. Of course, knocks and taps often have much more common, easily explained sources and causes.

The C-Bus position is that if you can respond with a knock, you can speak a reply or perhaps even show yourself. Though our position may seem like we expect too much from an entity, we believe expecting more or better quality responses likewise raises the quality of the phenomenon we acknowledge as evidence. From a scientific perspective, the evidence must be more substantive than a couple of knocks. Thus, when it comes to including versus excluding evidence, our motto is *When in doubt, throw it out*. It's our way of holding ourselves to a higher level of quality.

As we slowly made our way down the corridor, going room to room and taking our time in each of the spaces, we didn't detect anything unusual. When we entered the dining hall, though, we heard the rustling of curtains from one of the rooms we had just explored. We backtracked, yet found nothing was out of place.

Gradually, we worked our way to the dining hall, where a tired, old piano rested. I thought perhaps I could stir things up with a couple of chords. Here's a little ditty John produced for the team website.

bit.ly/ghostlyencounters-bell

Then, as if in response, right on cue it happened! We heard it clear as day, quite loud in fact: Brad Paisley. *Oh no*, I thought.

Yes, it was party time in Kimbolton, Ohio! Kitty-corner across the street, the party officially started. With no place to go and not much to do on a Saturday night, I guess a bonfire, beer, and loud country music from a garage stereo seemed natural.

John and I cussed in unison. Moments later, Chris came in, steaming and muttering a few choice words of his own. We went to the windows, where we saw a dozen people looking back at us, waving and swigging beer, followed by the most obnoxious sound a paranormal investigator ever wants to hear: the mocking, warbling woo-Ooo-ooo!

It was as if the air got sucked out of the room. Not even 10:00 p.m. and it appeared the locals were going to have some fun at our expense! We were all muttering expletives. Yes, it was infuriating, but there wasn't much we could really do about it. After all, this was their town, not ours. Both teams assembled at the nurse's station and we all commiserated.

One member from Chris's team suggested a parley: "Ask them to turn it down or we'll kick their asses." As enticing as the suggestion was . . . definitely not a good idea.

As I've said, patience is a requirement for paranormal investigating, so we decided to wait them out. Maybe they would eventually get bored or drunk or both—and turn their attention to more satisfying forms of entertainment someplace else.

They were extremely persistent.

I don't want to give you the wrong idea. Though we were in fact waiting for the beer and boredom to work its magic on the un-neighborly neighbors, we weren't wringing our hands, sitting there stupidly, waiting for the music to suddenly stop. We continued the investigation the best we possibly could, considering the circumstances. Still, all the audio was contaminated, and as the clock advanced from 12:00 a.m. to 2:00 a.m. and the roosters began to crow with no signs of the neighbors letting up, it became abundantly clear this investigation was a bust.

By 3:00 a.m., their numbers had slightly diminished, and a few were sleeping in lawn chairs, the music and volume unchanged. At 5:00 a.m., under the cover of darkness and unnecessarily loud music, we slipped out of Kimbolton and left that debacle of an investigation where it belonged: in the middle of Nowhere, Ohio.

I bear no animosity for the un-neighborly neighbors of the Bell Home. Whether the party was a regular event or whether the locals were partying on our behalf is irrelevant. Either way, stuff happens, requiring investigators to adjust or simply chalk it up to experience and move on, which is precisely what John and I did. By 6:00 a.m., we were southbound on I-77, exhausted from doing nothing and looking for a rest stop where we could get some sleep before completing the five-hour drive to Radford, Virginia, and St. Albans Sanatorium.

After catching a few hours of sleep at an Interstate rest stop, it was time for us to push farther south along I-77 to Virginia through some exceptional scenery. Though my frequent trips to Ohio from Atlanta have provided me an intimate familiarity with I-75 through the mountains of northern Georgia, Tennessee, and the rolling hills of Kentucky, few eastern routes are as dramatic and breathtaking as the forested Appalachian and Blue Ridge Mountains of West Virginia, Virginia, and the Carolinas, particularly on a bright, cloudless day. The truth is, photographs simply don't do justice to the spectacular scenery that surrounds that ribbon of highway.

St. Albans Sanatorium

Nestled on a hilltop in southwestern Virginia, overlooking the New River and the college town of Radford, looms the ominous St. Albans Sanatorium. Built on land first inhabited approximately fifteen thousand years ago by prehistoric Native Americans— on through the settlements of the Powhatan, Shawnee, and Cherokee nations, to early colonialism, Civil War engagements and on into modern times, everything in this region exudes history. The hillock where St. Albans quietly rests is no exception.

On this bluff, where Union cannonades rained death and destruction on Confederate settlements below (the Battles of New River Bridge and Cloyd's Mountain), cornerstones were placed, and in 1892, St. Albans (Lutheran) Boys School opened for business.

As magnificent as the St Albans Boys School was, it had its share of darkness. An article describing the school sums up some of the horror that plagued the intellectual students;

"The atmosphere at the school was rough and competitive. It clearly favored the stronger boys (or bullies as we would say today) and made short work of the more cerebral types like one E. Blackburn Runyon, whose painful experience at the school was poignantly summed up by a yearbook editor in 1904: 'E. Blackburn Runyon did not return after Christmas, much to our sorrow, as it put a stop to the football games on the terrace in which he figured prominently as the football.'" Though no official records indicate that students lost their lives (by suicide or by homicide) it is rumored that several lives were lost during the time that St Albans was a boy's school. http://stalbans-virginia.com/history.

In 1915/1916, the school and its associated fifty-six acres were sold to Dr. John King, who renovated and converted the school into the St. Albans Sanatorium—where, like Edinburgh Manor in its earliest years, the additional acreage was used for raising livestock and crops, "providing diversional exercises and employment . . . all of which are interesting and helpful to the patients."

Though the sanatorium was a financial struggle from the onset, Dr. King gradually expanded the facility to include more standard or traditional medical services to the community. By all accounts, St. Albans was in fact a success, providing much-needed physical and mental health services to the entire region. Patient numbers steadily grew, and by 1945, St. Albans had treated more than 6,500 patients, administered by a staff of forty-eight.

In the 1990s, the hospital was purchased by Carilion Health Systems and moved to a modern facility. The building and its associated acreage were gifted to the Radford University Foundation, and the building was scheduled for a date with the wrecking ball. Fortunately, concerned local citizens stepped in and in 2007 successfully halted the demolition in order to conduct a proper federally mandated historical review, effectively saving the grand structure . . . at least for the time being. At present, there are no plans for demolition.

St. Albans was a much-needed, much-valued asset to the region, and with its establishment and success occurring at the height of the Progressive Era, a time when industry, science, technology, education, and medicine were transforming, we likewise see a shift in perspectives on mental health and approaches to treating mental illnesses. Ironically, this is when and where the history of places like St. Albans darkens.

It's important to note that as the United States emerged from the Gilded Age (1869–1900), America lagged far behind Europe in the world of medicine. Though the practice of antiseptic surgery—first introduced by Great Britain's George Lister in 1865—had become widely practiced abroad, most American doctors and surgeons had yet to recognize the connection between hygiene and sanitary practices in terms of infections and disease. Perhaps the greatest achievements in American medicine at the turn of the century occurred at medical schools and colleges and in the way physicians were taught. Thus, in the early years of the twentieth century, we see a sudden explosion in the number of hospitals and clinics, not the least of which were psychiatric facilities.

During those years, it was believed that psychiatric disorders and mental illnesses were curable, setting the stage for an extensive period in medical history that was both enlightening and tragically barbaric. Naturally, hindsight is twenty-twenty; and if we knew then what we know now, we could have avoided horrendous experimental procedures like insulin shock therapy, where large doses of insulin were injected into patients to induce comas; or hydro therapy, where restrained patients were immersed in ice-water baths with the hopes of shocking the system and senses back into a state of normalcy. There were also lobotomies, where the frontal lobes of the brain were scarred with surgical instruments to calm anxious patients; and electroconvulsive (a.k.a. electro-shock) therapy, where electrical current is passed through the brain.* All these procedures were developed with the hope of "curing" a variety of mental illnesses, ranging from depression to schizophrenia. All of these procedures were practiced at St. Albans.

Grotesque and barbaric? Certainly, from our modern perspective. However, we cannot forget that the incredible advances in science, medicine, and our understanding of mental health did not spontaneously occur; they required extensive research and have advanced at an incredible rate over the past

---

* Though maligned in movies and television and likely misused in its earliest years (1930s through 1950s), highly refined forms of ECT are still in use today.

fifty years. As inhumane as these methods seem to us now, they were once cutting edge, conceived and experimented with in order to solve baffling psychiatric problems that continue to challenge us today.

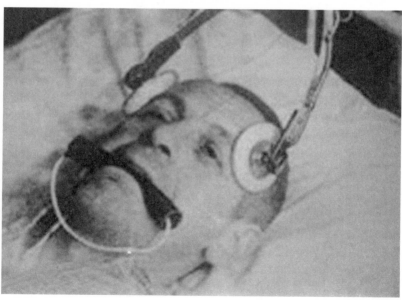

We arrived late in the afternoon, and the town appeared abandoned. Summer semester had not started yet, and for a Sunday, there was very little traffic or activity. After a couple of wrong turns around campus, we finally found ourselves crossing the New River, with the imposing St. Albans looking down on us. With a couple of hours to spare, we afforded ourselves the luxury of a decent sit-down meal where we commiserated about our previous night in Kimbolton.

Despite the Kimbolton investigation being a bust, we'd actually had a good time meeting and working with Ohio Lost Souls Paranormal. John also noted that he was looking to make some changes to the C-Bus team, and shake loose some deadweight members. I had a feeling Chris was going to play a role in those future plans. This was going to be a very busy year for C-Bus Paranormal. Along with completing this book, John also had an ever-growing list of locations he wanted to schedule.

After dinner, we made our way back to St. Albans, which, sitting as it did on a lonely hilltop in a deserted college town, presented an even stronger sense of desolation. As we waited for the arrival of Matt Slozer and the Autumn Moon Paranormal team, we walked the perimeter of what was truly a behemoth of a building.

As indicated by the banner at the front of the building, St. Albans was looking for a few good zombies—to work and perform in their annual haunted house. Obviously, the folks responsible for managing St. Albans were getting as much use out of the building as possible in order to preserve it from the wrecking ball. Operating a haunted house in a haunted sanatorium is certainly a viable means of generating revenue during the Halloween season. It also created some interesting moments during the course of the investigation.

Not long after our arrival, Matt and his team also arrived. Besides leading Autumn Moon Paranormal, Matt produces a Sunday night paranormal Internet radio show that I accidentally stumbled upon several months earlier: Dead Air Paranormal, on blogtalkradio.com. Based on a few of the shows I had listened to, I had an appreciation for his perspective on investigating and reviewing (accepting/rejecting) purported paranormal phenomena. I am also very much interested in

Matt's working hypothesis involving statistical analysis. Based on data and evidence collection at sites he has investigated multiple times, Matt believes that by documenting and analyzing the individual events or phenomena (residual versus intelligent; cordial versus malevolent) and where they specifically occur, over time valuable patterns and information will emerge from the data. This type of analysis may provide insights into the identification and behaviors of specific entities. As one of his preferred investigating locations (this was his fourth investigation at St. Albans), we were certainly interested in observing Matt and his team work and in learning what additional data he might collect. On this night, he would be broadcasting a segment of his Internet radio program live, allowing listeners to listen in on EVP and spirit box sessions.

Though structurally sound, St. Albans's interior spaces (halls, corridors, common areas, rooms, and treatment rooms) range from good to very rough condition, with many of the walls punched out, cut out, or pulled out. There was also tons of graffiti everywhere. It was impossible to tell if the interior damage was created for the haunted house effect, was part of renovation plans such as updating electrical service, the result of vandalism (when the building was abandoned), or in some of the smaller rooms . . . from physically aggressive patients.

With such an immense structure, setting up the DVR would be impractical, so we assembled the mobile night-vision camcorders, loaded up the backpack with accessories, and followed Matt and his team up to the third floor. This was the men's residential wing, where Autumn Moon prepared for their blog-radio program.

John and I proceeded deeper into the unsettling quiet.

I have to confess, St. Albans really unnerved me, making me feel extremely guarded and defensive. Blend equal parts background knowledge with physical darkness and complete disorientation, and I would challenge anyone, even the biggest skeptic, to *not* be fearful. Pushing deep into the building, we meandered past small employee bedrooms, and then doubled back to a short corridor and tight stairway that took us down to the second floor and a series of long corridors lined on both sides with heavy doors that, at one time, locked only from the outside.

We slowed our pace and began exploring each of the rooms, which were little more than 10-foot x 12-foot cells. During our initial tour, we had been told that these rooms served as both patient rooms and isolation (padded) cells. Here in these cramped, empty black spaces, true horror, reflected from history and the imagination, sets in.

The *vibe* of St. Albans was unlike anything I have previously experienced in these adventures, with an underlying feeling of mistrust. Along with the death and despair that naturally accompanies a hundred–year-old psychiatric facility that was overpopulated and understaffed, there was also a palpable feeling of the anger and pain associated with what we now readily label as abuse and neglect. With these thoughts in mind, we introduced ourselves to the anguished darkness, acknowledging the torments of the past and validated—to the best of our meager abilities—the wrongness of the methods and treatment that so many were forced to endure. This made one particular bit of evidence we collected all the more remarkable.

bit.ly/ghostlyencounters-stalbans

From the isolation cells of the men's wing, we moved on to a larger common area at the end of the corridor frequently used for group counseling sessions; the building remained stone-cold silent. Again, we encouraged whatever spirits that were present to join us and communicate. It is in these black and silent places, where you can barely see the nose in front of your face and can hear only your own breathing, that your eyes can play tricks on you.

Up to this point, I have been reticent to elaborate on some of the more circumstantial personal experiences I have had in haunted locations. In the world of paranormal investigating, a *personal experience* is an undocumented event or occurrence. The most common of these types of experiences are physical, such as being touched; or visual, such as seeing a shadow or apparition. Though some of these experiences can be extremely profound to the individuals who witness or experience them, we are reluctant to elaborate on these experiences beyond casual conversations and informal discussions.

Why are we reluctant? Because (1) the event is personal, typically limited to a single individual; and (2) it is undocumented by corresponding or corroborating audio or video evidence. Though group experiences have been reported and to some extent are qualitatively stronger, as a team we still feel the lack of supporting audio or video evidence makes the experience no less circumstantial.

Consequently, I have tried to limit the narrative to experiences that are supported by the evidence we share. Seeing things that I cannot support with evidence is essentially asking you, the reader, to *believe me* that it happened. By virtue of the fact that you are reading this text, I trust that you do in fact generally believe me. However, when I am unable to support my experiences, such as things that I saw—or thought I saw—I feel I am imposing on the trust I have tried to establish with you.

I apologize for this digression. I suppose it's my way of telling you that I did see things at St. Albans, things that I can't corroborate. What did I see? In this group counseling/sitting area, I saw a shadow—a subtle, vaguely human-sized area of deeper darkness that seemed to peek out from the last padded cell, then duck back in. It did this twice in the span of about ten minutes. Was it paranormal—a ghost or spirit? Quite possibly, but it might also have been a "floater" in my eye (see "eye floater" at webmd.com). It was one of those all-too-common events in paranormal investigating when you rub your eyes and do a double take. Honestly, I don't know what I saw, but I saw something—or *thought* I saw something—that both teased and troubled me. Why "teased"? Because it showed itself twice. Why "troubled"? Because I can't corroborate it, and that is the most frustrating thing of all.

With his radio program complete, Matt and his team joined us in the basement area where, strangely enough, a small two-lane bowling alley was immediately adjacent to the shock and hydro therapies rooms.

Electroconvulsive Therapy Room

Hydro Therapy Room

In this space, we participated with Matt as he conducted a spirit box session. As previously noted, a spirit box (a.k.a. Frank's Box) is a small, battery-powered device that operates on the same principle as a police scanner, basically racing through AM or FM radio frequencies, picking up signals. In paranormal investigating, it is believed that ghosts will or can communicate through these devices directly or in the white-noise background they create, uttering single words or short phrases.

Though the C-Bus team does have a spirit box as part of its arsenal, it is not a staple of our core investigating tool kit; we tend to be a little old school. What I found extremely interesting was how Matt used the spirit box, asking entities to repeat random words such as "apple." Hearing the random word repeated, in my opinion, goes a long way toward minimizing what I will call "the coincidence factor", the chance that the device picks up a word from an AM radio station that, by sheer coincidence, answers the question an investigator asks. For example:

Q: Are you here with us now?
A: Yes

~versus~

Q: If you're here with us now, say the word "apple."
A: Apple

As an investigator who tries to maintain a healthy sense of skepticism, particularly in matters of the evidence we obtain, hearing the word "apple" in response to my question carries much more weight than the simple "yes" reply. Why? Because the chances of the device picking up the "yes" from a DJ, a song, or commercial is far greater than picking up the word "apple."

Our time went fast in the gloom of St. Albans, and by 3:30 a.m., we had reached our physical limit and the end of the investigation. Cleanup was fast, and John and I were back on the road by 4:00 a.m. John went north and I went south, with each of us finding the first available roadside rest area to pull over and get some sleep before our respective long hauls back home.

In spite of the uncomfortable vibe of St. Albans and our nervous apprehension, we were both a bit disappointed in the results of this investigation. Though we did return with a few bits of evidence, I had expected more or better results from a place with such a dark history. Maybe that says more about me than it does about St. Albans. Here is the evidence we obtained.

bit.ly/ghostlyencounters-stalbans

Trans-Allegheny Lunatic Asylum

With a name like Trans-Allegheny Lunatic Asylum, there's no ambiguity what this place was for or about. These were not poorhouses, orphanages, or medical hospitals; they were facilities for the mentally deranged . . . the insane. What paranormal investigator (in their right mind) could pass up the opportunity to investigate one of America's most renowned, perhaps even notorious, warehouses for the insane? Seemed like a perfect finishing touch for my introduction to the world of paranormal investigating.

Asylums like TALA, and there are many of these places across the country (some still in operation), are truly remarkable historical artifacts. Examining them in the literature and in person provides a fascinating glimpse into our nation's past and our societal views about dealing with mental illness, more so in fact than places like St. Abans. Everything about TALA, from its location to its layout and architecture, was carefully thought out, designed, and planned to achieve a maximum effect for the patients who lived there. Within these plans, we see how early nineteenth-century *dark age* treatment of the mentally ill evolved into a more humane, dare I say enlightened, period of medical history. Sadly however, that period of enlightenment would not last.

Constructed between 1858 and 1881, prior to and at the outbreak of the Civil War (a remarkable story unto itself that includes the founding of the state of West Virginia), the Trans-Allegheny Lunatic Asylum (subsequently West Virginia Hospital for the Insane—1863; subsequently Weston State Hospital—1913) and institutions like it were the result of reform movements that began in Europe and gradually made their way to the United States. Chief among American reformers were people like Dorothea Dix and Thomas Story Kirkbride.

Dorothea Dix (1802–1887) was a teacher, author, and nurse who was instrumental in the radical reforms in the treatment of prison convicts and the mentally ill, who were traditionally housed together. After observing the widespread mistreatment and abuses suffered by both populations, particularly the indigent insane (such as being chained naked to a prison wall), she became a staunch and vocal advocate for the voiceless and defenseless.

Thomas Kirkbride (1809–1883) was a Quaker physician whose early work with the mentally ill in New England brought him to prominence in the early part of his career. Influenced by reforms made by Quakers in England and *moral treatment*: a philosophy based in dignity, compassion, and isolation. Rather than treating the mentally ill as criminals, the *moral treatment* promoted comfortable living in isolated environments, intellectual stimulation, and physical activities.

"There is no reason why an individual who has the misfortune to become insane, should, on that account, be deprived of any comfort or even luxury . . ."
Thomas Story Kirkbride, 1854

Besides the compassion provided to patients under his direct care, Kirkbride's ideas would ultimately coalesce into what became known as "The Kirkbride Plan," which called for the construction of large sprawling facilities in remote, isolated areas where patients could enjoy more freedom of movement and engage in meaningful mental and physical activities—all of which were considered both beneficial and curative. Kirkbride buildings consisted of large, richly appointed central administration centers, with long, staggered, multifloor extensions or wards radiating out from the central hub. The design provided ample sunlight, fresh air, and interior space promoting a more free and relaxed environment.

The Kirkbride Plan ultimately influenced many of the great architects of the time such as H. H. Richardson who designed Trinity Church in Boston, and landscape architect Frederick Law Olmsted who designed New York's Central Park, both of whom also designed and built state asylums. The contract for TALA ultimately went to Richard Snowden Andrews, a young up-and-coming antebellum architect. By all accounts, it appears TALA was one of Andrews's first major design projects. His later design work would include the Maryland Governor's Mansion in Annapolis and the south wing of the US Treasury Building.

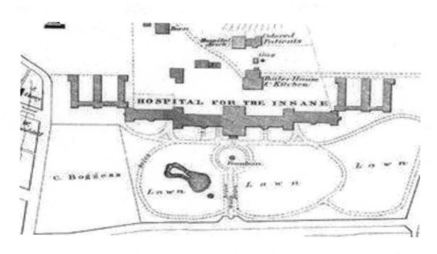

It is interesting to note that after serving as an artillery commander for the Confederacy and being severely wounded several times, Andrews was appointed by Jefferson Davis as an envoy to Germany where he successfully arranged the purchase of guns and munitions. Were it not for the surrender at Appomattox Court House a few days after Andrews's transaction in Germany, the outcome of the Civil War might have been very different. But I digress . . .

On twenty-seven sprawling acres in the isolated Appalachian town of Weston, West Virginia, the massive Trans-Allegheny Lunatic Asylum (two-tenths of a mile long) was built. Despite its immense size (242,000 square feet), TALA, in accordance with the Kirkbride Plan, was specifically designed to house a maximum of 250 people. Though its founding mission and early practices were noteworthy and noble, neither the mission nor the facilities could be effectively sustained, and by the late nineteenth century, the cracks were beginning to show.

By the 1890s, these institutions were all under siege. Economic considerations played a substantial role in this assault. Local governments could avoid the costs of caring for the elderly residents in almshouses or public hospitals by redefining what was then termed

"senility" as a psychiatric problem and sending these men and women to state-supported asylums. Not surprisingly, the numbers of patients in the asylums grew exponentially, well beyond both available capacity and the willingness of states to provide the financial resources necessary to provide acceptable care. But therapeutic considerations also played a role. The promise of moral treatment confronted the reality that many patients, particularly if they experienced some form of dementia, either could not or did not respond when placed in an asylum environment.
—Patricia D'Antonio, PhD, RN, FAAN; "History of Psychiatric Hospitals."

As the Kirkbride Plan began to crumble, perspectives on treatment of the mentally ill also began to change. With an ever-increasing understanding of neuroscience and brain function, focus shifted from moral and environmental treatment to medically based approaches, such as chemical/drug therapies and physical or sensory treatments, such as lobotomy, and electroconvulsive and hydro treatments.

As the pendulum swung, the grand architectural triumphs like TALA fell into disrepair, quickly decaying into hellholes for those unfortunate enough to be committed. By the 1950s, TALA held 2400 people in dreadfully overcrowded, ever deteriorating conditions. By the 1970s and '80s, with newer facilities and treatment methods, TALA's population at last began to decline. Finally in 1994, the massive facility was closed for good.

 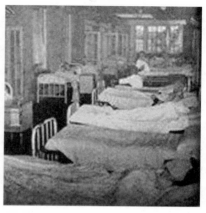

Above and on previous page: These images are **not** from TALA/Weston
State Hospital. They are instead from "A Pictorial Report
On Mental Institutions In Pennsylvania" (1946) and
have been included to give an idea of what overcrowding might have looked
like at TALA.

Unfortunately, Publisher's Clearinghouse hasn't shown up at either one of our doors, making the $1,750 cost ($1,500 admission plus $250 liability insurance waiver) for a private investigation at the Trans-Allegheny Lunatic Asylum impossible. We therefore had to jump on a public ghost hunt with lord knows how many other people. But hey, it was TALA . . . very much a heavyweight in the pantheon of paranormal locations. Thus, in the waning days of August, conveniently coordinated with getting my son back to college, we packed up the car with all his stuff and headed back to Cincinnati . . . by way of Weston, West Virginia.

This time, things would be a little different. Since I was coming north with my son in tow and the investigation would conclude promptly at 4:00 a.m., I wasn't going to be catching Zs on the side of the road in Nowhere, West Virginia. This was a job for Holiday Inn Express! While I was creeping around TALA, junior could luxuriate in the comfort of Weston's finest accommodations, and when I was finished with TALA . . . or TALA finished with me, I could at least get a few hours of sleep in comfort before hitting the road once again.

John and new C-Bus affiliate Christopher Oles, from Ohio Lost Souls Paranormal, arrived later that afternoon, and after a relaxed dinner at a local steakhouse, we returned junior to the hotel and loaded up our portable equipment for a quick drive through downtown Weston.

The Trans-Allegheny Lunatic Asylum is an impressive, imposing, and intimidating sight. After driving through tiny Weston, it is also easy to see why this behemoth facility was such an important economic anchor to the community and why Weston has never really recovered from TALA's closing back in 1994. However, on the warm summer night of our investigation, TALA was astir with a growing collection of investigators and paranormal enthusiasts, patiently waiting to be *admitted* . . . to see what they would find in the empty wards and corridors.

As we waited for check-in to begin, we milled around the main entrance, taking pictures and conversing with other participants. In retrospect I have to confess that for one who tries to pride himself on maintaining reasonable expectations, I think I fumbled the ball on this one. Although it was a public hunt, I had hoped that participant numbers would be low and thus have an ideal environment for some good audio or video captures. My hopes and expectations were not realistic and that was my fault. It was a warm August night at the last-gasp of the summer vacation period; I, in fact, was literally in the process of returning my son to college.

I don't want to give you the wrong idea or impression; there were not hundreds of people waiting to enter and experience the asylum. To the contrary, in total there were approximately a hundred people total, not a large number for such a sprawling complex. And in fairness to our friends at TALA, they cap their numbers (just like at OSR) to very reasonable levels.

At last, the doors were opened and we were allowed to file in, checking in at a computer station where four desktops allowed participants to confirm registration and e-sign the liability waiver. IDs were manually checked by staff volunteers, and we were finally allowed to enter the front foyer and adjacent rooms, which were originally used for office and administrative personnel, now restored and serving as museum space and a gift shop. The restoration gave a remarkable feel to the place while providing both interesting and disturbing exhibits of TALA's active years.

About thirty minutes later staff members called the assembled to order and directed those who signed up for the medical building ghost hunt, a separate option that centered on TALA's adjacent medical, geriatrics, and forensics buildings, to follow another staffer who led them away. This brought the numbers down to approximately fifty people, which put my mind at ease.

When we initially made our reservations, we felt it was probably best to begin in the main "Kirkbride" building. It's interesting to note that most investigators who have visited TALA return to explore both the main Kirkbride building (ghost hunt option #1), and the adjacent medical/geriatrics buildings (option #2) on multiple occasions—like Autumn Moon's Matt Slozer, who is making a statistical analysis of TALA. Matt has investigated the Kirkbride building five times and the outlying medical buildings thirteen times. Of course, the medical buildings remain on the C-Bus bucket list and we look forward to returning very soon.

A few moments later, those of us who remained were divided into four smaller groups and assigned a guide who would lead us throughout the building. We were assigned to Robert, a fellow who has been on staff at TALA for four years. Robert explained that he would lead us throughout the facility for the duration of the hunt; we would essentially work our way throughout the building as a group, ward by ward, spending approximately two hours on each floor. We would then rotate to another floor and progress through the building. Since the main entrances were locked, we were not allowed to leave the building unless it was absolutely necessary. After pointing out the bathrooms, smoking areas, and emergency exits, Robert led us into Ward One, where our adventure began.

TALA is an incredible facility, whose skilled staff and trained volunteers have done an equally incredible clean-up and restoration. This is especially true on the first floor, where a few administrative common areas and upscale physician accommodations have been repainted and furnished with period decor, quickly transporting visitors back to the early twentieth century.

TALA: Doctor's Lounge
http://weekendroady.com/2014/08/22/ghostly-travel-a-
trip-to-the-haunted-asylum/

TALA: Patient Sitting Room
Reprint courtesy of Jordan Hawk; jordanlhawk.com/

TALA: wheelchairs
Reprint courtesy of Jordan Hawk; jordanlhawk.com/

TALA: Ward One hallway
Reprint courtesy of Jordan Hawk; jordanlhawk.com/

Of course, the farther you walk from the central administrative center, the deeper you descend into TALA's darkness—where well-appointed work and common areas give way to desolate and decayed rooms for the sick and deranged. Judging by the silence of our group, I am sure everyone felt the same nervous apprehension I was feeling— uncertainty and fear.

TALA: window Reprint courtesy of Jordan Hawk; jordanlhawk.com/

TALA: View of Tuberculosis Ward from the Kirkbride (main) Building. http://splinteredkernels.com/2013/10/21/ west-virginia-part-2-serenitys-atrophy/

As we made our way to our first stop, the Civil War wing, we passed through Wards One and Four, where the bedridden and wheelchair-bound were housed. Robert explained that the squeaks of gurneys and roll of wheels against the tile floor are the most common phenomena experienced by staff and visitors. Though the unseen, unexplained sounds made by these pieces of medical equipment could certainly be distressing to some, he went on to explain that Ward One was generally less active and certainly less sinister than other areas we would visit. Naturally, our audio and video equipment were recording.

TALA: Fire Door to Civil War wing
https://barbmorrissey.wordpress.com/2014/06/04/
trans-allegheny-lunatic-asylum/

From the main corridor, we passed through an old-style fire door that separated the Kirkbride building from the Civil War wing—an extension of the main building that was its first structural element, only partially completed at the onset of the war in 1861. When the first shots were fired at Fort Sumter, Union forces from Ohio quickly descended on Weston, seizing the property and confiscating most of the currency at the Weston branch of the Exchange Bank of Virginia, taking an estimated $27,000.00 in cash. Meanwhile, back at the asylum construction site, the area was quickly converted for military purposes and renamed Fort Tyler; the partially completed extension was converted into barracks, while the foundation of the main Kirkbride Building was used as stables. During the ensuing war years, Weston and Camp Tyler proved to be valuable real estate, with possession changing from Union to Confederate hands several times.

Here and now, the space that once housed both Union and Confederate soldiers is simply open. However, the darkness that fills that space is unlike any gloom or shadow anywhere else in the building . . . black as ink, with an unshakable cold.

TALA: Civil War wing; exterior and interior
https://www.flickr.com/photos/itinerant_wanderer/5141085144/
in/set-72157625359329295

Robert explained that the most common paranormal activity in this area was the sound of footsteps and whispering. These occurrences, which have become legendary in this wing, are generally attributed to a Civil War soldier who has since been named Jacob. Why Jacob? According to volunteers, when asked to identify himself during ghost box sessions conducted in the wing, the name Jacob has been mentioned or repeated on several different occasions. Though I personally tend to be a little skeptical of spirit box responses and completely disregard anything the Ovilus word generator has to say, Jacob is as good a name as any when referencing the male spirit that resides in the wing. Besides, I tend to think that if everyone was constantly getting the name wrong, there would likely be an EVP of the spirit setting us straight.

With the tour and discussion of the first floor complete, Robert invited the group to wander and investigate the first floor at our leisure. John Chris, and I quickly peeled away from the group, returning to Ward One, away from the others. Hopefully, we could get some "quality quiet" before other investigators and enthusiasts in our group began filtering back into the ward. This was essentially how the evening proceeded: advancing through discreet areas of the complex as a group, provided the opportunity to investigate, then moving on to another area.

I very much understand and appreciate the balance owners (or nonprofit organizations) who operate these massive buildings must take by maximizing the number of people in each tour. Though dedicated investigators seek the quiet of small groups, owners understandably have little choice than to find the balance between satisfying investigators and maximizing admissions. More people equal more dollars for professional staffing and building renovations.

In cases like TALA or OSR (Ohio State Reformatory), hardcore investigators who can't afford a private investigation and choose to collect evidence during a public ghost hunting event must likewise be extremely discriminating of what they deem as evidence and publish as such in the public domain.

Rather than provide a floor-by-floor description of the asylum, I will instead share what I consider the highlighted areas, where a heightened creep factor and higher levels of reported paranormal activity correspond with the sad and horrific realities that make TALA one of the most haunted, if not *the* most haunted asylum in the United States.

Before taking a closer look at some of the madness and sadness that defines TALA, it's worth noting some of the causes or reasons why a person could be admitted or committed to an asylum like TALA.

REASONS FOR ADMISSION
1864 TO 1889

INTEMPERANCE & BUSINESS TROUBLE	DISSOLUTE HABITS
KICKED IN THE HEAD BY A HORSE	DOMESTIC AFFLICTION
HEREDITARY PREDISPOSITION	DOMESTIC TROUBLE
ILL TREATMENT BY HUSBAND	DROPSY
IMAGINARY FEMALE TROUBLE	EGOTISM
HYSTERIA	EPILEPTIC FITS
IMMORAL LIFE	EXCESSIVE SEXUAL ABUSE
IMPRISONMENT	EXCITEMENT AS OFFICER
JEALOUSY AND RELIGION	EXPOSURE AND HEREDITARY
LAZINESS	EXPOSURE AND QUACKERY
MARRIAGE OF SON	EXPOSURE IN ARMY
MASTURBATION & SYPHILIS	FEVER AND JEALOUSY
MASTURBATION FOR 30 YEARS	FIGHTING FIRE
MEDICINE TO PREVENT CONCEPTION	SUPPRESSED MASTURBATION
MENSTRUAL DERANGED	SUPPRESSION OF MENSES
MENTAL EXCITEMENT	THE WAR
NOVEL READING	TIME OF LIFE
NYMPHOMANIA	UTERINE DERANGEMENT
	VENEREAL EXCESSES

© Trans-Allegheny Lunatic Asylum

Reprint, courtesy of Trans-Allegheny Lunatic Asylum

...And some more reasons,

OVER ACTION OF THE MIND	VICIOUS VICES
OVER STUDY OF RELIGION	WOMEN TROUBLE
OVER TAXING MENTAL POWERS	SUPERSTITION
PARENTS WERE COUSINS	SHOOTING OF DAUGHTER
PERIODICAL FITS.	SMALL POX
TOBACCO & MASTURBATION	SNUFF EATING FOR 2 YEARS
POLITICAL EXCITEMENT	SPINAL IRRITATION
POLITICS	GATHERING IN THE HEAD
RELIGIOUS ENTHUSIASM	GREEDINESS
FEVER AND LOSS OF LAW SUIT	GRIEF
FITS AND DESERTION OF HUSBAND	GUNSHOT WOUND
ASTHMA	HARD STUDY
BAD COMPANY	RUMOR OF HUSBAND MURDER
BAD HABITS & POLITICAL EXCITEMENT	SALVATION ARMY
BAD WHISKEY	SCARLATINA
BLOODY FLUX	SEDUCTION & DISAPPOINTMENT
BRAIN FEVER	SELF ABUSE
BUSINESS NERVES	SEXUAL ABUSE & STIMULANTS
CARBONIC ACID GAS	SEXUAL DERANGEMENT
CONGESTION OF BRAIN	FALSE CONFINEMENT
DEATH OF SONS IN WAR	FEEBLENESS OF INTELLECT
DECOYED INTO THE ARMY	FELL FROM HORSE IN WAR
DERANGED MASTURBATION	FEMALE DISEASE
DESERTION BY HUSBAND	DISSIPATION OF NERVES

© Trans-Allegheny Lunatic Asylum

Reprint courtesy of Trans-Allegheny Lunatic Asylum

This is some pretty bizarre stuff here! *Causes* and *symptoms* of insanity were wide, diverse, and often times completely subjective. Though legitimate mental and physical handicaps could lead to a committal, family members—usually the male head of the house—could just as easily commit a spouse or a child to an asylum, often with little or no supporting evidence. The truth is, in the nineteenth and early twentieth century, society operated from a completely different set of norms. Back in the day, American society was male dominated, and women, frequently referred and characterized as the *lesser* or *softer* sex, were treated as such. In the realm of the asylum, it often took little more than the accusation of an angry husband or father to commit a wife or family member. A husband wanting to pursue an affair with another woman needed to do little more than simply drop off his spouse at the asylum, claim some completely fabricated symptom or malady, and effectively dispose of her—anywhere from a few months to a few years—to a lifetime.

Naturally, many of the committals were justifiable. With little understanding of conditions like Down syndrome and autism (conditions once referred to as mental retardation), we can understand how or why even loving family members felt helpless in providing for the afflicted. Of course, not all committals were reasonable or justified, and based on the menu of causes listed above, some motives were (by today's standards) completely criminal. Want to access your wife's inheritance? Drop her off at the hospital. Tired of dealing with a troublesome child? Drop him or her off at the hospital. Tragically, this all-too-common practice of integrating healthy and sane individuals with the legitimately insane destroyed lives and turned well-intentioned institutions into hellholes.

Even in institutions as large as TALA, it is heartbreaking to consider the existence of a Children's Ward, which was located on the second floor. Could a child find a measure of happiness and joy in this place? Perhaps in the early days, but as the patient population began to expand in the 1920s and 1930s and explode in the 1940s and 1950s, God only knows how good . . . or how bad, life could be for a child within these massive walls. Yet now, in the twenty-first century, the occasional voice or laugh of a child can be heard and sometimes recorded within these halls and quiet rooms.

With three cemeteries and literally thousands of burials, mostly in unmarked graves, death was not uncommon in the asylum. Though disease and epidemic were the most common causes of death in TALA, murder was also known in these now-quiet halls. TALA legend tells of a nurse who went missing and was discovered months later, her body stuffed under a back staircase. Another legend tells of a patient-against-patient murder, where the victim was stabbed seventeen times and bled out while crawling to the nurses' station.

TALA: Unrestored second floor Children's Ward
Photo courtesy of Jordan Hawk www.jordanlhawk.com

Perhaps the most horrific murder in TALA's dark past surrounds two patients ganging up and killing a third patient in the not too distant past; HIPPA laws prevent us from identifying the victim and the assailants. Though the murder is a matter of historical record, specific details are a bit sketchy. In one account, the assailants brutally beat their victim to death. In the second and far more gruesome account, it is said that after beating their victim senseless, the assailants attempted to hang their victim with bedsheets. When the hanging failed to achieve the desired result, the killers dragged their victim to a nearby bed and crushed his skull under a steel bedpost. When questioned about their motives, the ringleader is said to have explained, "He was taking up my oxygen."

Do these ghosts still reside in TALA? There are many people who believe they do. What about a child named Lily or an invalid woman named Ruthie? Who's to say, and can we ever really know for certain?

I tend to think along the lines of Robert, who noted when we discussed the number, the nature, even the identity of TALA's many ghosts.

Though our devices and technology are beginning to give us indications of who these people were, I don't know if we'll ever be certain. I think what's more important is that despite the tragic circumstances and even horrors that took place here, this was still the only home many of the residents and patients ever knew. That had to be of some comfort to those who lived here and many who died here. There's no question, there are many ghosts here at TALA, and that shouldn't shock or surprise anyone. After all, where else did they know, where else would they go?

bit.ly/ghostlyencounters-tala

Epilogue

~~~~~~~~

"What a long, strange trip it's been."
—*Jerry Garcia*

W hen I look back on that warm summer night when I first
ventured into the municipal cemetery and caught those very
first EVPs, then think about where I am now and where I have
been most recently, it's hard not to wax a little nostalgic. At first,
I was just curious to see for myself if these things called ghosts,
and paranormal investigating in general, were for real. Now I
communicate with investigators across the country, in an effort
to find new places to explore and new strategies to improve my
investigating skills. It has been a long, strange trip.

As I re-reviewed the evidence presented here, as well as other
clips from the C–Bus files, and evidence clips out in cyberspace
posted by a variety of investigating teams, my mind went off on

a minor tangent, prompting me to call my son at college. After the usual catching-up on money, grades, and girls, I gave him a math problem to help me solve; he's the numbers wizard, and I . . . do everything else (math was not my content area). I asked him: what is two minutes out of eight hours, percentage-wise? After about twenty seconds of scratching out some math, he came back with 0.417 percent.

Naturally, he asked what these figures meant. I explained that, conservatively speaking, two minutes represents the average amount of audio evidence collected during an average eight-hour paranormal investigation at a haunted location. "Oh," he replied politely. I could almost hear him rolling his eyes. Of course, I take this with a grain of salt, coming from a kid who watches Japanese language anime cartoons and doesn't know a lick of Japanese.

Obviously, the greater point is the proportion of time spent conducting an investigation relative to the amount of evidence obtained. Like so much of this field, it's really quite remarkable. Of course, each paranormal team judges their evidence differently; some are more inclusive of what they define as evidence, and some teams (like C-Bus) are much more conservative. But even the most liberal of teams would be hard-pressed to argue the math.

So, why do investigators do this when the results are so . . . scant? Though I can't speak for other teams, I know why the C-Bus team does it. It is in that 0.147 percent of time that the real meat and potatoes of what we do lie. It's a conundrum wrapped in an enigma because the answer is another freaking question!

I believe investigators spend eight hours investigating to extract two minutes of evidence for a couple of reasons. First, I believe we do it because we don't know what we are going to find, but we do have a lot of ideas and we want to test out those ideas whenever the opportunity allows. We know the phenomenon is energy-based, and we believe that these entities somehow draw or extract electromagnetic energy from the localized environment and sometimes even from our devices. But we don't know how they convert that energy into words or phrases that our devices can pick up, or how they manifest themselves into visible shadows and apparitions.

Though there are clearly scientific principles at play here, such as the Law of Conservation of Energy (i.e., that energy cannot be created or destroyed, only transformed), we're left with the why. Why do these events, these phenomena, take place at all? To consider the *why*, we must consider another aspect of paranormal inquiry that is no less fascinating but equally perplexing—enter the psychics and mediums. Although I know this area of paranormal curiosity provides answers and comfort to some, there are just as many people who are believers, some that are very uncertain, some that are dubious, and some who simply scoff. Sounds like the scientific community debating man-made global warming.

The simple fact remains: the evidence obtained during these investigations represents human-based interactions. We ask a question or seek validation, and *they* reply in a manner that is either verbally or physically understandable to us. Unfortunately for us, it seems that 90 percent of the time we can only hear their voices through our devices. Can someone please tell us what the hell is going on here?

Of course, we assume that the *they* we are referring to, the ghosts or spirits, are the post-life remnants of people: what survives after the body dies. Are these entities the *soul* or *spirit* of a person, and if it is, is it measureable?

Back in the early twentieth century, Dr. Duncan MacDougall, a Haverhill, Massachusetts, physician, conducted a study to determine whether the human body lost weight at the moment of death—the supposition being that the human soul has mass and that at the point of death the soul departs or escapes the body. For his study, MacDougall constructed a lightweight bed that was placed on a highly sensitive platform beam scale and observed the death of six individuals. It's a fascinating story in science history that produced some interesting results. Though MacDougall acknowledged that his sample population was small, the experiment not without technical and procedural issues, and recognizing that many more studies needed to be conducted, he observed that at the time of death, test subjects generally lost about an ounce of weight. Could this be that energy transformation?

The scientific community ultimately discarded and discredited McDougall, but a Pandora's box had been opened. Was MacDougall's experiment revisited and repeated? It appears so, and the subject certainly warrants further reading. Generally speaking, it does, however, seem that once the body dies, traditional mainstream science has no further interest in us . . . as humans, other than cause of death and the rate and manner our bodies decay. Here, in fact, lies the great disconnect. It seems that mainstream science is far more comfortable pooh-poohing the ethereal concept(s) of the human soul or spirit. Personally, I take great solace knowing that throughout recorded history, many of humanity's greatest minds, thinkers, and scientists were once labeled heretics, only to be recognized decades or centuries later for their knowledge and insights. Is there a Copernicus among us? I can only hope so.

SOUL HAS WEIGHT, PHYSICIAN THINKS

Dr. Macdougall of Haverhill Tells of Experiments at Death.

LOSS TO BODY RECORDED

Scales Showed an Ounce Gone in One Case, He Says—Four Other Doctors Present.

Special to The New York Times.

BOSTON, March 10.—That the human soul has a definite weight, which can be determined when it passes from the body, is the belief of Dr. Duncan Macdougall, a reputable physician of Haverhill. He is at the head of a Research Society which for six years has been experimenting in this field. With him, he says, have been associated four other physicians.

Dr. Macdougall's object was to learn if the departure of the soul from the body

New York Times; March 11, 1907

And though the naysayers continue to *nay*, investigators rightly continue their fun and spooky adventures, pumping dollars and support into haunted locations throughout the United States—preserving, remembering, and experiencing the decaying corners of our history and the ghostly remnants of the people who made it.

Appendix 1

~~~~~~~~~

Haunted Directory

Please note: You must always acquire the proper permission before investigating any location. Public and private properties must be respected at all times, and many "ghost hunting" groups have been arrested and prosecuted for trespassing by not acquiring the owner's consent. This is for your safety and all other parties involved.

The information contained in this appendix was obtained from a variety of sources, and as such, the authors make no claim to the accuracy of any of the entries contained therein. It is ultimately the reader's responsibility to effectively research each location for specific information and instructions.

Alabama

Sloss Furnaces: Birmingham
http://www.slossfurnaces.com

Sloss Furnace is a historic landmark and a testament to the industrial age. However, over time the structure has also become rather well known for its ghostly inhabitants. There have been over sixty documented worker deaths at the location, and many believe that some of their restless spirits still roam the property.

Alaska

Historic Anchorage Hotel: Anchorage
http://www.historicanchoragehotel.com

The Historic Anchorage Hotel is believed to be haunted by the victim of an unsolved crime. Anchorage's first police chief was found murdered—shot in the back with his own weapon on February 20, 1921. The crime itself happened within a few feet of the building, and it's rumored that his spirit returns to the scene of the crime each year still seeking justice for his murder. There have also been sightings of a female spirit in a white dress, objects moving by themselves, and even the sounds of children running down the hallways.

Arizona

Bird Cage Theatre: Tombstone
http://www.tombstonebirdcage.com

The Bird Cage Theatre opened its doors on December 25, 1881. The establishment featured a saloon, gambling parlor, theatre, and a brothel. During the building's years of operation there were at least twenty-six deaths related to gun or knife fights within the theatre. It's not surprising that the building now seems to boast a plethora of ghostly sightings.

Jerome Grand Hotel: Jerome
http://www.jeromegrandhotel.com

This former hospital is said to be haunted by many spirits, and sadly the building itself bore witness to several deaths within its walls. Some of the building's main reports of activity seem to center around an elevator accident, a woman in white, and a child that has been seen running through the bar area. It's not uncommon for the hotel guests to report doors closing by themselves, footsteps, and even objects moving on their own accord.

Arkansas

Crescent Hotel: Eureka Springs
http://www.crescent-hotel.com

The Crescent Hotel has been called "America's Most Haunted Hotel," and it has been given this nickname for a variety of reasons. The building originally opened its doors in 1886 as a resort for the rich and famous, and at one point was even being used as a college. In 1937 the hotel was purchased and converted into a hospital and health resort. Unfortunately, the new owner turned out to be a scam artist who had previously been run out of Iowa for practicing medicine without a license. He had claimed that he had found the cure for numerous ailments, including cancer, and would constantly lash out at organized medicine, which he accused of being corrupt and profit-driven. Eventually the owner would do jail time for mail fraud before losing possession of the building.

The basement is a hot spot among paranormal tours as it had previously been used as the morgue while the hospital was in operation. There are also believed to be at least eight spirits that call the property home, and some are believed to be the poor souls that had hopes of finding their miracle cure.

California

Alcatraz: San Francisco
http://www.nps.gov/alcatraz

This infamous maximum-security prison is simply known as "the rock," and it's been featured as the topic of discussion for several major motion pictures. It's not uncommon for visitors and guests to have their own paranormal experiences while visiting this secluded island. There have been several reports of disembodied voices, cell doors slamming shut, and phantom footsteps.

RMS *Queen Mary*: Long Beach
http://www.queenmary.com

The RMS *Queen Mary* is a retired ocean liner that has now become a historical treasure. The *Queen Mary* made its maiden voyage in 1936 and sailed until 1967. Oddly enough, the ship has since become a magnet of paranormal activity with sightings of past sailors, a lady in white, and voices of children within the ship's nursery.

Winchester Mystery House: San Jose
http://www.winchestermysteryhouse.com

The Winchester Mystery House is a 140-room mansion built by Sarah Winchester. Oddly enough, most of the doors and stairways of this location lead to nowhere, and the house itself is a remarkable oddity of a twisted maze. The most common belief is that Sarah kept building on to the home in an attempt to hide from the ghosts of all the people killed by her late husband's line of Winchester rifles. However, in a strange turn of events, it is believed Sarah's spirit now haunts this labyrinth of a mansion.

Colorado

Stanley Hotel: Estes Park
http://www.stanleyhotel.com

The Stanley Hotel is perhaps one of the most infamous hotels in the United States, and it was built in 1909 by Freelan and Flora Stanley of the Stanley Steamer fortune. The building was originally a resort for the couple to entertain guests during their extended vacations in Colorado, and many guests believe that they never truly left the hotel after their deaths. Flora Stanley was known to be a piano player, and there have been reports of the piano in the ballroom playing by itself. There have also been reports of full-body apparitions on the premises and the occasional sound of children within the hallways.

Connecticut

Captain Grant's Inn: Preston
http://www.captaingrants.com

Captain Grant's Inn dates back to 1754 and has quite a complex history. Revolutionary War soldiers were once garrisoned at the Inn, and slaves were housed at the Inn during the Civil War. There have been several reports of paranormal activity at the inn, and most of them are focused around the "Adelaide Room." There was once a guest who reported waking up in the middle of the night and seeing a colonial-era woman holding hands with two children by her bed. There have also been reports of objects being moved and phantom footsteps in the attic.

Delaware

Fort Delaware: Delaware City
http://www.destateparks.com/park/fort-delaware

The historic Fort Delaware is now believed to be haunted by
the spirits of Confederate soldiers who were captured in the
Civil War. Many visitors have claimed to have experienced full-
bodied apparitions, cannon fire, and disembodied voices.

Florida

Castillo de San Marcos: St. Augustine
http://www.nps.gov/casa/index.htm

The Castillo de San Marcos is dated back to 1672 and is the oldest
masonry fort in the United States. There have been frequent
reports of visitors seeing the spirit of an unknown woman and
several Spanish soldiers roaming the grounds of this historic fort.

Riddle House: West Palm Beach
http://www.southfloridafair.com/yesteryear-village

The Riddle House was built in 1905 and was used as a funeral
parlor in the beginning stages of its history. The building was then
converted to a private residence in the 1920s. There are reports of
an angry ex-employee who committed suicide at the location by
hanging himself in the attic. His spirit is believed to still haunt the
property, and he has been known to lash out at visitors.

St. Augustine Lighthouse: St. Augustine
http://www.staugustinelighthouse.org

The St. Augustine Lighthouse was built in 1824 and is believed
to have several spirits still taking residence on the property. There
are various paranormal claims featuring the lighthouse's original

owner, a caretaker, and two girls who tragically died near the property in a drowning accident. There have been reports of children laughing, footsteps, the smell of cigar smoke, and full-bodied apparitions in the lighthouse and its nearby museum.

Georgia

Moon River Brewing Company: Savannah
http://www.moonriverbrewing.com

In 2003, the American Institute of Paranormal Psychology named Savannah the most-haunted city in America, and the Moon River Brewery is Savannah's most-known, haunted location. The brewery was built in 1821 as a hotel, and it was also used as a hospital during Savannah's numerous yellow fever outbreaks. Hundreds of people died, mostly children, on the upper floors of the building during these outbreaks. There have been reports of visitors seeing spirits of children in the brewery and also of malevolent entities that have been reported to cause physical attacks.

Hawaii

The Nu'uanu Pali Lookout: Honolulu
http://dlnr.hawaii.gov/dsp/parks/oahu/nuuanu-pali-state-wayside/

One of the bloodiest battles in Hawaii's history occurred at the Pali Lookout. In 1795 the battle of Nu'uanu took place pitting future King Kamehameha's army against Chief of Oahu Kalanikupule's army. Eventually Kalanikupule's forces were defeated with the culmination of the battle taking place at the edge of the Pali Lookout. Kamehameha's warriors forced Maui chief Kalanikupule's men to their deaths off the side of the cliff. An estimated four hundred warriors died in the battle, and their ghosts are said to haunt the Pali at night. Visitors have reported seeing apparitions of ancient Hawaiian soldiers being tossed off the cliff during park hours.

Idaho

Old Idaho State Penitentiary: Boise City
http://history.idaho.gov/old-idaho-penitentiary

The Idaho State Penitentiary opened its doors in 1872 and quickly gained notoriety as being one of the most violent penitentiaries in America. The prison became a war zone with constant riots and problems with overcrowding and eventually became decommissioned in 1973. Visitors to the old penitentiary often report seeing shadow figures and hearing disembodied voices while roaming the structure's old corridors.

Illinois

Bachelor's Grove Cemetery: Midlothian
http://bachelorsgrove.org

Bachelor's Grove Cemetery is an abandoned graveyard near Chicago with fewer than two dozen of its two hundred tombstones remaining. There are also beliefs the graveyard used to be a dumping ground for the victims of Chicago's organized crime family, but there hasn't been any supporting evidence provided to prove this theory. The most common reports of activity at the cemetery involve balls of light, full-bodied apparitions, and near collisions with a ghostly vehicle.

Peoria State Hospital: Bartonville
http://www.peoria-asylum.com

The Peoria State Hospital has been in operation since 1902 and has also been called the "Illinois Hospital for the Incurable Insane" and the "Illinois General Hospital for the Insane" during its winding history. This old psychiatric hospital was known for taking patients characterized as "incurable," and many people believe that some of the patients decided to stay long after their deaths. The asylum's visitors have reported disembodied voices, shadow figures, the sounds of crying, and full-body apparitions during the asylum's tours and investigations.

Indiana

Thornhaven Manor: New Castle
https://www.facebook.com/ThornhavenManor

The foreboding structure known as Thornhaven Manor is believed to have been built around 1845 and is thought to have been a stop on the Underground Railroad. Some of the home's prior residents were Civil War soldiers, and others became victims in a fiendish murder conspiracy plot. The house has seen its share of turbulent history and has recently been saved from the wrecking ball.

Whispers Estate: Mitchell
http://www.whispersestate.com

Whispers Estate is a beautiful 3,700 square-foot Victorian home located in Mitchell, Indiana. It's believed to have been built in 1894 and has been dubbed one of the most terrifying homes in America. Various paranormal phenomena have been experienced in the home, and there have been reports of apparitions, footsteps, voice phenomenon, unexplained smells, and shaking furniture.

Iowa

Edinburgh Manor: Scotch Grove
http://edinburghmanor.wix.com/edinburgh

Edinburgh Manor sits deeps in the heartland of Iowa and was built on the same land as the former "Jones County Poor

Farm." The poor farm itself was in operation from 1850–1910 and bore witness to at least eighty documented deaths. In 1910 the poor farm was demolished, and Edinburgh Manor took its place. Edinburgh Manor was originally constructed to house the incurably insane, the poor, and the elderly. The building stayed in operation until November of 2010. The most common claims of paranormal activity in the building include female disembodied voices, footsteps, and shadow figures.

Villisca Ax Murder House: Villisca
http://www.villiscaiowa.com

The Villisca Axe Murder House has a reputation for being one of the most haunted homes in America, and this is due to the unsolved crime that was committed at the house in 1912. Josiah Moore and his family were found brutally hacked to death in their home by an unknown assailant on the morning of June 10th. A bloody axe was determined to be the murder weapon, and it was found in the downstairs bedroom next to the parlor. The victims were Josiah Moore, Sarah Moore, their four young children, and two neighbor children who were staying the night. The crime itself was never solved despite a few suspects going to trial for the murders. To this day investigators and visitors have reported the disembodied voices of children, doors closing by themselves, and a malevolent entity that some believe resides in the attic.

Kansas

The Sallie House: Atchison
http://www.thesalliehouse.com

The Sallie House is known for being extremely active, and it has perhaps taken on the title of the most haunted location in Kansas. There are various reports of full-bodied apparitions, physical attacks, and moving objects from the house's visitors and investigators. The activity itself is claimed to be quite intense, and has previously driven former owners out of the home.

Kentucky

Perryville Battlefield: Perryville
http://www.perryvillebattlefield.org

The Perrysville Battlefield was the stage for the biggest Civil War battle in Kentucky. On October 8, 1862, the Union and Confederate forces collided in a fierce battle for control. The end result would see a combined estimate of 7,600 soldiers killed or wounded. Many visitors have reported seeing spectral soldiers and large balls of light on the battlefield. There have also been claims of visitors hearing residual gunfire and cannon blasts during the park's normal tours and investigations.

Waverly Hills Sanatorium: Louisville
http://www.therealwaverlyhills.com

The historic Waverly Hills Sanatorium originally opened its doors in 1910 to help with the tuberculosis outbreak and would then expand to a larger facility by 1926 due to the demand. Individuals that had contracted tuberculosis were normally isolated away from the general public, and sanatoriums were commonly built so the subjects would have a place to rest and get plenty of fresh air. Waverly Hills stayed in operation until 1961 when the disease could finally be treated with an antibiotic. The building was then renovated and turned into the Woodhaven geriatric hospital. Woodhaven would stay in operation until 1981 when it was closed by the state.

Waverly Hills Sanatorium today is known for being a hotbed of paranormal activity, and the building itself has been on several paranormal television shows. Thousands of people died within the walls of Waverly Hills Sanatorium, and many believe that some of those unfortunate souls are still on the property. The building's normal paranormal claims involve full-bodied apparitions, shadow figures, unexplained lights, and disembodied voices.

Louisiana

Myrtles Plantation: St. Francisville
http://www.myrtlesplantation.com

The Myrtles Plantation was built in 1796 and is known across the country as a paranormal hot spot. However there has been some inconsistency from the legends being passed down and of how many murders have actually occurred at the plantation. At this time the only documented murder came from a man who was shot on the porch of the house by an unknown assailant. There were, however, a number of deaths in the home as a result of the yellow fever epidemic. To this day, visitors continuously report sightings of what is believed to be the spirit of an African American woman wearing a green turban, spirits of young children, and a grand piano that is believed to play by itself.

Maine

Kennebunk Inn: Kennebunk
http://www.thekennebunkinn.com

The Kennebunk Inn in Maine was built in 1799 and is believed to be haunted by two spirits. One spirit is thought to be of a prior owner, and the other is believed to be a former clerk of the establishment. Alleged paranormal activity in the Inn includes glasses falling off shelves, objects being moved, and disembodied voices.

Maryland

Antietam National Battlefield: Sharpsburg
http://www.nps.gov/anti/index.htm

The Battle of Antietam is known for being the bloodiest one-day battle in American history. Twenty-three thousand soldiers were killed, wounded, or missing after twelve hours of savage combat on September 17, 1862. It's not surprising that the battlefield itself is reported as being haunted. Visitors normally report seeing spectral soldiers and also of hearing phantom gunfire.

Massachusetts

Lizzie Borden House: Fall River
https://lizzie-borden.com

The Lizzie Borden House was built in 1889 and is now a popular bed and breakfast. However, the home wasn't as inviting to its past residents. Former owners Andrew and Abby Borden were found murdered in the home in 1892 due to multiple blows to the head with an axe. Oddly enough the main suspect in the crime was Andrew's daughter Lizzie Borden. Lizzie was arrested a week after the killings and faced trial three months later. She was acquitted.

USS Salem: Quincy
http://www.uss-salem.org

The USS Salem is a former navy cruiser that has been opened to the public as a museum. The ship itself has seen many voyages, and at one time served as a hospital after the 1953 Ionian Earthquake. Many believe that the spirits that roam the ship were victims from when the ship was in service.

Michigan

Traverse City State Hospital: Traverse City
http://www.thevillagetc.com

The Traverse City State Hospital opened its doors in 1885 as the Northern Michigan Asylum for the Insane. This is the final Kirkbride plan asylum standing in Michigan, and it doesn't look as ominous as some of the other Kirkbride asylum designs from the past. The building itself went through extensive renovations as of late, and is being refurbished for residential and commercial development.

In its years of operation the asylum was run under a different philosophy, and it was often referred to as "beauty is therapy." They believed that love, fresh air, community, and purpose were the roads to returning sanity to patients. However, most of these statements still fail to mention that this hospital also performed lobotomies and electroconvulsive therapy in extreme cases. The paranormal claims for the former asylum include full-bodied apparitions of adults and children, and disembodied voices and screams.

Minnesota

Palmer House Hotel: Sauk Centre
http://www.thepalmerhousehotel.com

The Palmer House Hotel is a unique historic site that was built over the ashes of another former hotel. The Sauk Centre House burned to the ground in 1900, and this provided the opportunity for a new first-class hotel to be built in its place. Oddly enough there were no fatalities from the original fire, but many believe the spiritual aspect of the hotel comes from two suicides that happened on the property. Particularly rooms number 11 and number 17 have been reported as the most active within the establishment.

Mississippi

Monmouth Plantation: Natchez
http://www.monmouthhistoricinn.com

The Monmouth Plantation was built in the year of 1818 and believed to be haunted by General John A. Quitman, who bought the home in 1826. The plantation has recently gone through a series of renovations, and it's believed that the spirit of John Quitman has been watching over the efforts. The general's apparition is said to still be wandering the floors of the plantation and has been seen dressed in full uniform by guests.

Missouri

Lemp Mansion: St. Louis
http://www.lempmansion.com

Lemp Mansion is an intriguing yet ominous mansion located in St. Louis, Missouri. The mansion itself is said to be haunted by members of the Lemp family, who made their mark in the brewing industry after arriving from Germany. The family itself suffered great tragedies, and four subsequent family members committed suicide in the early 1900s. Each death was by pistol, and three were under the same roof. It's been reported that visitors of this now bed and breakfast often have their own ghostly encounters with the spirits of the Lemp family.

Missouri State Penitentiary: Jefferson City
http://www.missouripentours.com

The Missouri State Penitentiary opened its doors in the year of 1836 and was once the largest prison in the United States.

The prison itself has also earned a nickname over time as "the bloodiest forty-seven acres in America" due to the prison's excessive amount of violence. The prison has been host to several popular paranormal television shows and is now available for tours and paranormal investigations. The most common paranormal activity reported in the prison seems to involve full-bodied apparitions and unexplained noises.

Montana

Montana State Prison: Deer Lodge
http://www.pcmaf.org/wordpress

The Montana State Prison was in operation from 1871 until the late 1970s. Similar to most prisons, it has seen its share of executions, riots, and violent deaths. The solitary confinement area is said to be particularly active as visitors frequently report the feeling of being touched and in some cases pushed. Other paranormal reports include disembodied voices and phantom footsteps.

Nebraska

The Argo Hotel: Crofton
http://www.theargohotel.com

The Argo Hotel dates back to 1911 and originally opened its doors as a hotel. Eventually the hotel changed hands a few times and became a clinic for several years. The hotel was then sold to a new owner who renamed the building back to the Argo Hotel. During renovations the new owner discovered a burlap sack of infant bones within the building's basement wall. There has since been a stir of paranormal activity in the hotel with the most common reports being of a female apparition, and a man seen in what appeared to be a hospital gown on the property.

There have also been reports of female disembodied voices, the sound of children crying, and glasses shattering by themselves on the bar.

Nevada

Old Washoe Club: Virginia City
http://www.thewashoeclub.com

The Old Washoe Club dates back to the 1870s and was a bar for the wealthy men of its time. There was also a brothel on the upper floors of the bar, and its past is believed to be causing some of the hauntings within the building. There is believed to be a spirit of a woman dressed in blue that sometimes appears on the staircase and another younger female that has been seen in the basement area. There is also another ghost in the building that is believed to have committed suicide at the establishment.

New Hampshire

The 1875 Inn / Tilton Inn: Tilton
http://www.thetiltoninn.com

The Tilton Inn is claimed to be haunted by a twelve-year-old girl named Laura. The girl is believed to have been burned alive during a fire when the building was a rooming house in the early nineteenth century. Visitors have frequently provided reports of seeing a young girl in their rooms, and this has often times startled unknowing guests. Recently there has been documentation provided that describes three different fires that have all occurred on the spot where the building stands today. There were no casualties reported in the fire of 1903. However, the casualties are unknown with the two previous fires.

New Jersey

Burlington County Prison: Mount Holly
http://www.prisonmuseum.net

The Burlington County Prison was originally opened in 1811 and closed its doors in 1965. The most common paranormal reports in the building involve a full-bodied apparition that is normally seen floating from the building's entrance to the yard outside, and there have also been reports of a taller entity often seen in the basement area. The third floor of the establishment is also believed to be a very active area for paranormal occurrences.

New Mexico

Luna–Otero Mansion: Los Lunas
http://www.lunamansion.com

The Luna–Otero Mansion is known for a haunting that is believed to be caused by former house mistress Josefita Otero. There have been reports of visitors seeing her as a full-bodied apparition that normally can be seen on the second floor of the establishment. Josefita also has been known to rock back and forth in an old rocking chair on the same floor.

New York

Rolling Hills Asylum: East Bethany
http://rollinghillsasylum.vpweb.com

The building now known as "Rolling Hills Asylum" was built in 1827 and was originally called the Genesee County Poor Farm. During its years of operation it was used for an infirmary, orphanage, tuberculosis hospital, and nursing home. There are also believed to be over 1,700 bodies buried in unmarked graves on the property itself.

The building is host to several paranormal claims including disembodied voices, doors slamming, footsteps, full-body apparitions, feelings of being touched, and shadow figures. The building is also known for its reports of a seven-foot shadow figure. Many believe this to be a former patient named "Roy" who was known to have a form of gigantism due to a pituitary disorder.

North Carolina

Carolina Inn: Chapel Hill
http://www.carolinainn.com

The Carolina Inn was built in 1924 and is said to be incredibly active. The most common reports of paranormal activity seem to revolve around a former guest at the establishment. After his retirement the man lived in room number 256 for over seventeen years until his death in 1965. This individual also appears to have been a prankster as he has locked multiple guests out of the room, opened blinds and curtains, and even rattled doorknobs. The hotel eventually installed electric doors to the former room after renovations occurred in 1990. However, the locks still get jammed from time to time.

North Dakota

Fort Abercrombie: Abercrombie
http://www.ftabercrombie.org

Fort Abercrombie was built in 1858 and was the first military settlement in North Dakota. The fort itself engaged in a few conflicts with the Indians in the area, and there were quite a few fatalities at the location. Visitors have reported hearing the sounds of battle and disembodied voices. There have also been reports of doors opening and closing of their own accord.

Ohio

Madison Seminary: Madison
https://www.facebook.com/pages/Madison-Seminary/
180590777832

The Madison Seminary was originally built in 1847 and opened its doors as a school for the Lake County community. It later housed families of Civil War victims, and then became a center for the Ohio Department of Mental Hygiene and Corrections. There have been many claims of paranormal activity reported within the building, including objects moving by themselves, disembodied voices of women and children, shadow figures, and full-bodied apparitions.

The following advertisement appeared in the 1993 newspapers for the Madison Seminary: "For Rent: Historic building on Middle Ridge Road ... can be leased cheap, caution ... building may be haunted."

Ohio State Reformatory: Mansfield
http://www.mrps.org

The Ohio State Reformatory opened its doors in 1896 as an intermediate prison, and the building stayed in operation until it was deemed unfit to operate in 1990. The location has gained worldwide fame due to its appearance in popular films and music videos, and paranormal investigators flock to the building each year in hopes of getting a glimpse of its world-renowned paranormal claims. There are several reports of activity from this prison, including disembodied voices, shadow figures, physical attacks, footsteps, and cell doors slamming by their own accord.

Prospect Place: Trinway
http://www.gwacenter.org

Prospect Place is a twenty-nine-room mansion built by abolitionist George W. Adams in 1856 and was once a prominent stop on the Underground Railroad. There are a few known deaths within the house, and the spirits of the dead are normally more than willing to speak with visitors. The most common reports of activity involve intelligent response EVPs, disembodied voices, footsteps, and occasionally full-bodied apparitions.

Oklahoma

The Skirvin Hotel: Oklahoma City
http://www.skirvinhilton.com

The Skirvin Hotel has been making quite a bit of news lately in the local community as reports continue to flood in about the building's paranormal activity. There is believed to be a female spirit in the establishment that has been causing quite a bit of ruckus by propositioning male guests. Objects in the hotel have also been known to move by themselves, and celebrity guests staying at the hotel have made reports to the local media about their encounters. There have been many legends and rumors of whom the spirit could be. However, to this point there hasn't been documentation to support her identity.

Oregon

Multnomah County Poor Farm: Troutdale
http://www.mcmenamins.com/edgefield/location

The Multnomah County Poor Farm was an old asylum for the elderly, disabled, and mentally challenged, and it's still in operation today as a hotel! However, to find it you would need to search for it under its new name McMenamins. Many people still believe that the current hotel is a hotbed for paranormal activity, and a female apparition has been seen in certain parts of the building. There have also been reports of what many believe to be the spirit of a dog and the sounds of children crying in what would have previously been the asylum's old infirmary section.

Pennsylvania

Eastern State Penitentiary: Philadelphia
http://www.easternstate.org

The Eastern State Penitentiary opened its doors in 1829 and is an impressive structure to see. There are claimed to be several spirits on the premises, and at one time even Al Capone was locked away in the prison. During his stay Al Capone believed that he was being haunted by James Clark, who was murdered in the St. Valentine's Day Massacre under Capone's orders. Cell block 12 seems to be a hot spot within the building, and visitors normally report seeing shadow figures and full-bodied apparitions. It's also not uncommon to hear the closing of cell doors and the occasional disembodied voice.

Farnsworth House Inn: Gettysburg
http://www.farnsworthhouseinn.com

The Farnsworth Inn dates back to 1810 and was in the middle of the Civil War cross fire between the Union and the Confederates. The home literally has over one hundred bullet holes through the side of the structure and is believed to have seen quite a bit of activity in the Civil War for both factions. The home is now a bed and breakfast, and visitors often report seeing a woman in 1800s' attire walking around the Inn. There have also been reports of phantom footsteps and the occasional apparitions of soldiers.

Gettysburg Battlefield: Gettysburg
http://www.nps.gov/gett/index.htm

The town of Gettysburg itself has an incredible amount of paranormal reports, and this of course is related to the battle of Gettysburg. The battle itself was fought for over three days in July of 1863 and was one of the most crucial battles of the Civil War. There are various hot spots on the battlefield with the "Devil's Den" and "Little Round Top" being favorites among tourists. It's not uncommon for visitors to see soldier apparitions, hear phantom gunfire, or experience intelligent voice phenomenon.

Hill View Manor: New Castle
http://www.hauntedhillviewmanor.com

Hill View Manor opened its doors in 1926 and stayed in operation until financial restraints closed it in 1994. The historic manor was once a nursing home, and several people passed away within its walls. Visitors, however, claim the old building is still active. Many of Hill View's former patients are believed to still roam the halls, and it's not uncommon to get a glimpse of the activity through tours and investigations. Paranormal activity reported at the manor includes shadow figures, disembodied voices, and hospital curtains moving by themselves.

Rhode Island

The Ladd School: Exeter
http://www.theladdschool.com

Ladd School was a home for the early twentieth-century feebleminded. It also seemed to become a warehouse for petty criminals, wayward females, and anyone else that was deemed of low character. It was believed that society was a better place with these individuals removed from the public.

The school quickly became known for its scandals involving forced sterilization, incarceration without trial, and employee misconduct until it closed its doors in 1993. Unfortunately the building is no longer available to the public due to its deterioration, but the town's locals still report hearing cries from the school to this day.

South Carolina

Old Charleston Jail: Charleston
http://www.nps.gov/nr/travel/charleston/old.htm

The Old Charleston Jail in South Carolina opened its doors in 1802 and stayed in use until 1939. In the jail's operational years it housed some of Charleston's most infamous criminals, nineteenth-century pirates, and Civil War prisoners. Visitors frequently report shadow figures, disembodied voices, and heavy doors that slam closed by their own accord.

South Dakota

Hotel Alex Johnson: Rapid City
http://www.alexjohnson.com

The Hotel Alex Johnson is starting to become well known for its paranormal activity, and for some reason the eighth floor is the most active section of the entire building. The most notorious ghost story involves a lady in white that is commonly reported in room 812. It is believed that a young lady either committed suicide by jumping to her death or was pushed out of the window of her room. Her spirit has been seen in the room and also occasionally in the hallway of the establishment. Other guests have also reported seeing the spirit of the hotel's founder, Alex Johnson, and an unidentified child.

<u>Tennessee</u>

Carnton Plantation: Franklin
http://www.carnton.org

Carnton Plantation was built in 1826 and was once used as a Confederate hospital site during the Civil War. Several visitors to the plantation have reported that some of the ghostly soldiers of the past still walk the grounds of the building to this very day. Their apparitions have been seen, and there have also been sightings of a female spirit dressed in white walking on the back porch of the estate.

Old South Pittsburgh Hospital: Pittsburgh
http://osphghosthunts.com

The Old South Pittsburgh Hospital is regarded as being one of the most paranormally active locations in all of Tennessee. The hospital stayed in operation from the years of 1958 to its closing in 1998. The land that the building now sits on also has its own tragic past. There is documentation of an old plantation that burned down to the ground (with seven known casualties), and it also felt the struggles of the Civil War in the 1800s. There are several spirits that are believed to haunt the old hospital, and the common reports of paranormal activity involve shadow figures and disembodied voices.

<u>Texas</u>

Yorktown Memorial Hospital: Yorktown
https://www.facebook.com/yorktownhospital

The Yorktown Memorial Hospital closed its doors in the 1980s, but many visitors claim that some of the deceased patients themselves didn't leave. There have been paranormal reports from visitors claiming to be attacked by an unseen presence, and shadow figures being seen within the hallways of the old hospital.

Utah

The Union Station: Ogden
http://theunionstation.org

The Union Station has been rebuilt a few times over the years due to age and fire damage. Unfortunately, it's also been the scene of a tragic train wreck known as the "Bagley Train Disaster." The wreck killed forty-eight people and injured another seventy-nine. The most common paranormal reports involve the spirit of a female who walks the upstairs hallways, footsteps, loud bangs, and the distinctive sound of children playing.

Vermont

Norwich Inn: Norwich
http://www.norwichinn.com

The Norwich Inn was originally built in 1797 and was purchased by Charles and Mary Walker in 1920. According to legend, Mary maintained the Inn's tradition as a tavern during the Prohibition Era and was believed to be selling bootleg liquor out of the basement of the tavern. Mary eventually died at the Inn, and it's believed that she still haunts the building. There have been reports of seeing a female apparition in a black dress around the top floors of the building, and she has also been frequently seen in the dining room area.

Virginia

St. Albans Sanatorium: Radford
http://stalbans-virginia.com

St. Albans Sanatorium is often described as the most-haunted location on the East Coast, and its reputation is starting to live up to the moniker. The building was originally opened in 1892 as the St. Albans Lutheran Boy School, but the land the building was sitting on had a history long before the structure was built. At one point the Powhatan, Shawnee, and Cherokee Indian tribes inhabited the land, and it was also used as a focal point in the Civil War. In 1865 Union forces defeated Confederate forces during the battles of Newbern and Cloyd's Mountain.

In 1916 the building was converted to a mental hospital and renamed St. Albans Sanatorium. It wasn't uncommon for patients to succumb to experimental treatments such as Insulin Coma Therapy, Electroconvulsive Therapy, and Hydro Shock Therapy. There were also a rather large number of suicides documented during the sanatorium's years in operation. St. Albans is home to several paranormal reports, including full-bodied apparitions, shadow figures, voice phenomenon, and at times physical contact.

Washington

Thornwood Castle: Lakewood
https://www.thornewoodcastle.com

In 1907, a wealthy individual named Chester Thorne purchased and dismantled a four hundred-year-old Elizabethan manor in England, and then had it shipped brick by brick to be included in the building of Thornwood Castle. The castle was truly a labor of love in which both Chester and his wife

Anna were able to hold grand garden parties and dinners for the likes of Presidents Theodore Roosevelt and William Howard Taft. Eventually both of the Thornes would perish in their remarkable home, and the castle stands today as a bed and breakfast. To this day visitors of the castle have frequently reported seeing the spirits of both Chester and his wife Anna on the property.

West Virginia

Trans-Allegheny Lunatic Asylum: Weston
http://trans-alleghenylunaticasylum.com

The former "Weston State Hospital" is one of the more unique locations that have been opened up to the public for paranormal investigations. The building itself is the largest hand-cut stone masonry building in North America and was originally designed to hold 250 people. However, by the 1950s the asylum became overcrowded and had an estimated 2,400 people living in generally poor conditions. The asylum had its share of conflict before it was even able to open its doors to patients. The west wing became a battleground between the Union and Confederate forces during the Civil War. The building was finally completed and opened for patients in 1864 and stayed in operation until 1994 when it was forced to be closed due to the physical deterioration of the facility.

Hundreds of patients died in the Weston State Hospital during its years of operation, and there are several reminders of their suffering still being felt throughout the building. Visitors and investigators have made several reports of full-bodied apparitions, shadow figures, physical attacks, disembodied voices, and hearing the sounds of children playing in the facility.

West Virginia State Penitentiary: Moundsville
http://www.wvpentours.com

The West Virginia Penitentiary has often been discussed as one of the most violent prisons in America. The prison opened its doors in 1876 and was in operation until 1995. Various methods of torture were implemented on unruly prisoners, and the prison also became the stage for several violent riots. The West Virginia Penitentiary also provided executions in the form of the electric chair and by hanging in the gallows. Visitors and staff believe that there are intelligent spirits at the location and also residual activity within the building. Full-bodied apparitions, shadow figures, and disembodied voices are now the most common claims of paranormal activity reported at the prison.

Wisconsin

First Ward School House: Wisconsin Rapids
http://www.relativelyhaunted.com

The First Ward School House was built in 1896 and was used in various schooling projects until it was abandoned in 1979. The building itself has been the focal point of several local legends and paranormal claims that seem to date back to when the school was still in operation. Most of these stories seem to focus on a boy named Oscar who is believed to have died on the property. The most common reports of activity include disembodied voices, shadow figures, footsteps, and the sounds of school desks being moved. However, it should also be noted that there are no longer school desks in the school.

<u>Wyoming</u>

Wyoming Frontier Prison: Rawlins
http://wyomingfrontierprison.org

The Wyoming Frontier Prison was in operation between the years of 1901 and 1981. It was the first state prison in Wyoming and held some of the state's most violent offenders. Back in those days there was no such thing as "prisoner's rights," and troublemakers would often be beaten or tortured within the walls of the prison. It's estimated that 250 people lost their lives within the prison walls, and it has seemed to cause a plethora of paranormal activity. Visitors have reported seeing full-bodied apparitions and hearing unexplained voices during tours of the property.

Appendix 2

~~~~~~~~~~

A National Directory of Paranormal Teams and Investigators

The purpose of including a national directory of paranormal teams and investigators is threefold: 1) to illustrate the widespread interest and popularity in ghost hunting and paranormal investigating; 2) to point enthusiasts interested in joining or starting their own team toward local or regional teams and resources; and 3) to provide some direction for individuals who are seeking validation and/or assistance with paranormal activity taking place in their home or place of business. The approximately 350 groups listed in this directory represent only a small fraction of the literally thousands of teams nationwide. Readers seeking to join a group or seek advice on matters relating to paranormal activity are strongly encouraged to conduct their own due diligence on any group they decide to interact with.If you are seeking assistance from any team or group, remember:

there are no recognized professional certifications or licensing agencies, and most groups do NOT charge for consultations or investigations.

The following teams have graciously given their permission to be included in the appendix of this book. We sincerely appreciate their participation, support, and contributions the field of paranormal inquiry.

ALABAMA		
Researching In Paranormal	Enterprise	facebook.com/ researchinginparanormal
Alabama Spirit Hunters	Holly Pond	alabamaspirithunters.com
Rocket City Paranormal	Huntsville	rocketcityparanormal.com
Mobile Order Of Paranormal Investigators	Mobile	mobileparanormal.com

ARIZONA		
Paramediacentral	Gilbert	paramediacentral.com
Route 66 Paranormal Investigators	Kingman	route66paranormalinvesti-gators.com
Ghosts Of Arizona, Paranormal Society	Mesa	ghostsofarizona.webs.com
ASN's The Trackers	Phoenix	asntrackers.com
Lone Wolf Para Investigations	Phoenix	gregpawlak.wix.com/ ghostblog

Phoenix Arizona Paranormal Society	Phoenix	phoenix-arizona-paranormal-society.com
Residual Effect Arizona Paranormal Entity Research Team (REAPER)	Phoenix	reaperteam.com
AzPrism Paranormal	Surprise	AzPrism.com

ARKANSAS		
River Valley Paranormal Research & Investigations	Fort Smith	rvpri.com

CALIFORNIA		
Amped Paranormal Investigations	Bakersfield	ampedparanormal.com
Western Region Paranormal Research	Ceres	wrpr-online.com
Halo Paranormal Investigations – HPI International	Elk Grove	jazmaonline.com
Sis Paranormal Society/Spirit Interventions Services	Fullerton	sisparanormalsociety. webnode.com
Vortex Hunters	Hemet	vortexhunters.com
Mystery Monitors Paranormal Society	Lancaster	galileanministries.org
Spirrit Paranormal	Los Angeles	spirrit.net

California Specialists In Paranormal Research	Monterey Bay	projectcaspr.com
Central Coast Paranormal Investigators	Nipomo	ccpinvestigators.com
Cal-Para Paranormal Research Organization	Redlands	calpara.org
South Bay Paranormal	Redondo Beach	ValentinaGhostGirl.com
Pacific Coast Paranormal Investigation	Riverside	pacificcoastparanormal. com
California Haunts Paranormal Investigation Team	Sacramento	californiahaunts.org
Pacific Coast Spirit Watch	Sacramento	pacificcoastspiritwatch.net
Paraxplorer Project	San Diego	paraxplorerproject.com
Santa Cruz Ghost Hunters	Santa Cruz	santacruzghosthunters. com

COLORADO		
Paranormal Research Association of Colorado	Boulder	colorado.praofb.org
Spiritbear Paranormal	Boulder	spiritbearparanormal.com

Culz Paranormal Investigators	Castle Rock	culzparanormalinvestigators.webs.com
Lockdown Paranormal	Denver	lockdownparanormal.com
Mountain Paranormal Investigations	Erie	mtnparanormal.com
Code 3 Paranormal	Lone Tree	code3paranormal.com
Socopi Paranormal	Pueblo West	SoCoPi.co

CONNECTICUT		
Lost Woods Society	Danbury	thedao.webs.com
Connecticut Skull And Spirit Paranormal	Enfield	ctskullandspiritparanormal.com

DELAWARE		
Delaware Paranormal Research Group	Felton	delawareparanormal.blogspot.com

FLORIDA		
Key West Paranormal Society	Boca Raton	keywestparanormalSociety.com
Pinellas/Pasco/ Paranormal Hostile Haunts Specialists	Holiday	pinellaspascoparanormal.com
Jacksonville's Researchers Investigating the Paranormal	Jacksonville	jprs-rip.com

P.O.I.N.T. Paranormal	Lake Worth	pointparanormal.com
561 Paranormal	Lantana	561paranormal.com
The Space Coast Paranormal Society	Melbourne	thescps.com
Haunted Apparition Hunters	Naples	hauntedapparitionhunters.com
Florida Paranormal Association	Ocala	fpa.name
Orlando Paranormal Investigations	Orlando	orlandoparanormal.org
The Beyond Investigators	Orlando	thebeyondinvestigators.com
The Ghost Tracker Paranormal Research & Tours	Ormond Beach	theghosttracker.com
Emerald Coast Paranormal Concepts	Panama City	emeraldcoastparanormalconcepts.com
Prospectors of the Paranormal	Sebring	midfloridaweb.com/paranormal
Lost Paranormal Indicators	St. Cloud	lostparanormalindicators.weebly.com
Aura Paranormal Investigations	St. Petersburg	auraparanormal.com
Spirits of St. Petersburg	St. Petersburg	spiritsofstpetersburg.com
Genesis Paranormal Services	Tampa	genesisparanormal.org

| Ghost Hunters Of South Tampa (GHOST) | Tampa | ghosttampa.com |
| The Phantom Realm Research Society | Thonotosassa | phantomrealm.com |

GEORGIA

Southeastern Institute of Paranormal Research	Atlanta	siprinvestigations.com
Newton Paranormal Society	Covington	http://newtonparanormalsociety.webs.com/
Timeless Paranormal	Lilburn	timelessparanormal.com
Southeast Paranormal Investigative Research Information Team	Moultrie	southeastern-paranormal.com
Southern Belles Paranormal Society	Resaca	southernbellesparanormalsociety.weebly.com

ILLINOIS

Mineral Springs Paranormal Research Team	Alton	mineralspringshauntedtours.com
HOPE Investigators	Antioch	hopeinvestigators.vpweb.com
Spirit Paranormal Investigative Research Intelligence Team	Bartonville	spiritghosthunting.com
Paranormal Anomaly Search Team	Bolingbrook	pastinvestigators.com

Zero Point Quantum Paranormal	Bolingbrook	zeropointparanormal.weebly.com
Sight: Southern Illinois Ghost Hunting Team	Centralia	sight–il.com
Champaign Urbana Paranormal Society	Champaign	cuparanormal.org
Chicago Researchers & Investigators of the Paranormal Theory	Chicago	criptheory.com
The Illinois Paranormal Group: In The Dark Investigations	Chicago	inthedarkinvestigations.com
Nexus Paranormal Investigations	Crystal Lake	nexuspi.com
New Age Paranormal Research	Decatur	newageparanormal.com
Effingham County Ghost Hunters Society	Effingham	effinghamcountyghs.wix.com/crossroadshauntings
Bump In The Night Paranormal Investigations	Joliet	bumpinthenightparanormal.com
Illinois Metaphysical & Paranormal Society	Mattoon	teamimps.com
Hunters of the Unknown	Minooka	huntersoftheunknown.com
Paranormal Research Society of Southern Illinois	Mt. Vernon	paranormal–research–society–southern–illinois.com

Illinois Ghost Seekers Society	Pekin	illinoisghost.com
Manifestation Investigations Ghost Hunting Team	Pittsfield	mightparanormal.webs.com
Midwest Ghost Society	Plano	midwestghostsociety.com
IL-MO Entity Trackers	Quincy	il-moentitytrackers.com/
Capital Area Paranormal Society	Springfield	capsinvestigations.com
McHenry County Paranormal Research Group	Woodstock	paranormalassist.com
All Seeing Paranormal	Worth	allseepara.com
VParanormal	Yorkville	vparanormal.com

INDIANA		
Griffith Paranormal Society	Griffith	griffithparanormalsoci-etygps.yolasite.com/
Indy 24/7 Paranormal	Indianapolis	indy247paranormal.com
P.I.O.T. (Paranormal Investigations & Observations Team)	Indianapolis	piotparateam.iconosites.com/
Paranormal Detectives of Indianapolis	Indianapolis	pdiindiana.com

Paragon Paranormal – Shadow Chasers	Paragon	paragonparanormal.com
Ask Mike Paranormal	Terre Haute	gotquestionsaboutghosts. yolasite.com#sthash. kE88OeTv.dpuf
Warsaw Indiana Paranormal Research Studies	Warsaw	wiprs.com

IOWA		
Cedar Rapids Paranormal Investigations	Cedar Rapids	crparanormal.com
Paranormal Iowa	Clarion	paranormaliowa. proboards.com
South Central Iowa Paranormal Investigative Team	Pella	scipit.com
Paranormal Endeavors	W. Des Moines	paranormalendeavors.com

KANSAS		
Beyond The Sunset Paranormal	Topeka	btsparanormal.com
Whispers in the Dark Paranormal Society	Valley Center	whispersitdparanormal. weebly.com/
Wichita Paranormal Research Society	Wichita	wichitaparanormal.com

KENTUCKY		
BlueGrass Ghost Chasers	Frankfort	bluegrassghostchasers.net
NexGen Paranormal Research	Bowling Green	nexgenparanormal.org
Ole Skool Paranormal	Madisonville	oleskoolparanormal.com

LOUISIANA		
Louisiana State Paranormal Research Society	Abbeville	lspr-society.com
Everyday Paranormal of Louisiana	Baton Rouge	everydayparanormalla.com
New Orleans Ghost Hunters	New Orleans	neworleansghosthunters.com
Louisiana Spirits Paranormal Investigations	Pineville	laspirits.com
Underground Paranormal Inc	Shreveport	undergroundparanorma.wix.com/upinc

MAINE		
Paranormal Reactions	Eliot	paranormalreactions.com
Paranormal Research Investigators of Southern Maine (PRISM)	Hollis Center	prism-me.org

MARYLAND		
Inspired Ghost Tracking	Glen Burnie	inspiredghosttracking.webs.com/
Scientific Investigation of Ghosts & Hauntings Team	Hagerstown	callsight.net
Chesapeake Paranormal Researchers	Hughesville	chesapeakeparanormalre-searchers.com
Serious Paranormal Investigative Society. (S.P.I.S.)	New Windsor	spiparanormal.com
Fairfield Paranormal Society	Taneytown	fairfieldparanormalsociety.com

MASSACHUSSETTS		
Massachusetts Paranormal Research Group	Attleboro	tmprg.com
Paranormal Research Association of Boston	Boston	praofb.org
RTS Paranormal Investigation	Franklin	rtsparanormalinvestiga-tion.com
Mass Ghost Hunters Paranormal Society	Gloucester	mghparanormalsociety.webs.com
East Coast Transcommunication Organization	Lowell	ectoparanormal.com

Whaling City Ghosts	New Bedford	whalingcityghosts.net
Consultants of Paranormal Research Organization	Osterville	copro39.com
Greater Boston Paranormal Associates	Pembroke	thegbpa.org
Boston Paranormal Investigators	Waltham	bostonparanormal.org

MICHIGAN		
GHS Paranormal Team	Farmington Hills	ghsparanormal.com
Michigan Spirit Quest	Flint	mispiritquest.com
Grand Rapids Ghost Seekers	Grand Rapids	grandrapidsghostseekers.com/
Michigan Paranormal Alliance	Grand Rapids	m-p-a.org
The Southern Michigan Paranormals	Kalamazoo	thesouthernmichiganpara-normals.com
Paranormal Investigations of Michigan	Lansing	parainmi.com
Michigan Paranormal and Cryptid Investigations	Mount Pleasant	mpci.weebly.com
Hauntech.net	Pontiac	hauntech.net

Spirit Chasers Ghost Hunters Society	Roseville	scghmichigan.wix.com/scgh
Shadow Paranormal Society	Traverse City	shadowpara.tk
Third Eye Paranormal Society	Westland	thirdeyeparanormalsociety.com

MINNESOTA

The Paranormal P.I'S	Champlin	theparanormalpis.com
Duluth Paranormal Society	Duluth	duluthparanormal.com
Dakota County Paranormal Society	Hastings	dakotacountyparanormal.com
Johnsdale Paranormal Group	Onamia	johnsdaleparanormal-group.com
Search4Spirits	Sartell	russvictorian.com/my_search4spirits.html
Central MN Ghosthunters	Spring Lake Park	centralmnghosthunters.com/
St.Croix Paranormal	Stillwater	stcroixparanormal.com

MISSISSIPPI

| Smoke & Mirrors Paranormal | Clinton | smokeandmirrorspi.weebly.com |
| Memphis Area Paranormal Research Organization | Senatobia | ghosthuntersmississippi.webs.com/ |

MISSOURI		
Moonlite Paranormal Investigations (SEMO)	Dexter	moonliteparanormal.com
Mid-Mo Supernatural League	Jefferson City	mid-mo-supernatural-league.webnode.com/
Kansas City Paranormal	Kansas City	kansascityparanormal.com/
Second Sight Ghost and Paranormal Investigation	Kansas City	ssgpi.com
Spookstalker	New Haven	spookstalker.com
D.A.R.K. Paranormal	Potosi	darkparanormal.wix.com/darkparanormal
Ozark Haint Hunters	Potosi	http://www.carrollscorner.net/OzarkHaintHunters.htm
One True Paranormal	Springfield	onetrueparanormal.com
The Ozarks Paranormal Society	Springfield	theozarksparanormalsociety.com
Moonlite Paranormal Investigations (STL)	St. Louis	moonliteparanormal.com

NEBRASKA		
Southeast Paranormal Investigators in Nebraska	Fairbury	spiin.org
TRIP Paranormal	Gretna	tripparanormal.com
Interstate Paranormal	Omaha	interstateparanormal.net

NEVADA		
Bigfoots Pad Paranormal	Las Vegas	bigfootspad.com/
Nevada Paranormal Task Force	Las Vegas	nevadaparanormaltask-force.com
The Mystery Gang	Reno	wix.com/mysterygang/of-nevada

NEW HAMPSHIRE		
SilentWhispers Paranormal Society	Bedford	silentwhispersparanormal-society.com
Paranormal Reactions	Dover	paranormalreactions.com
Paranormal Research Association of New Hampshire	Manchester	nh.praofb.org

NEW JERSEY		
Tri-State Paranormal Research		tsprghosts.com
Garden State Ghost Hunters	Brick	gardenstateghosthunters.com
East Coast Paranormal Research Organization	Colonia	ecopronj.com
Paranormal Activity Research Society	Farmingdale	parsinvestigations.com/

East Coast Research and Investigation Paranormal Team	Hamburg	ecriptghosthunters.com
Dusk Till Dawn Paranormal Investigators	Maple Shade	dusk-till-dawn.homestead. com/
Central Jersey Paranormal Research Group	Plainfield	cjprgroup.com
Jersey Unique Minds Paranormal Society	Salem County	jumps.2fear.com
Bearfort Paranormal	West Milford	bearfortparanormal.com

NEW MEXICO		
Los Muertos Spirit Seekers	Albuquerque	losmuertosspiritseekers. com
Ghost Paranormal Investigators	Cimarron	ghostparanormalinvestiga-tors.webs.com
Grave Concerns	Clovis	paraportal.wix.com/ graveconcerns

NEW YORK		
Paranormal Researchers of Niagara and Erie	Buffalo	pro-ne.org
PSI- Paranormal Scientific Investigators	Farmington	psiny.net
Regional Investigators of the Paranormal (RIP)	Lockport	riparanormal.blogspot. com

Paranormal Pursuit	New York	paranormalpursuit.com
SpiritVestigations	Newark	spiritvestigations.org
Dutchess Paranormal Investigators	Poughkeepsie	dutchesspi.com
Queensbury Paranormal Investigation Team	Queensbury	queensburyparanormal.com
Extreme Paranormal Encounter Response Team	Ravena	extremeparanormalteam.com
Long Island Paranormal Investigators	Ronkonkoma	liparanormalinvestigators.com
Uini Research	Scotia	uiniresearch.com
South Glens Falls Paranormal Society	So. Glens Falls	sgfparanormalsociety.com
Paranormal Investigations of Rockland County	Suffern	pirc-ny.com
Momentum Paranormal Investigators	Tonawanda	momentumparanormal.com

NORTH CAROLINA		
Enigma Paranormal Research & Investigation	Burlington	enigmaparanormal.com
Camel City Spirit Seekers	East Bend	camelcityspiritseekers.yolasite.com/#/

Supernatural Research Society	Elkin	srsocietync.webs.com
Paranormal Chasers	Fremont	paranormalchasers.com
The Paranormal Detectives	Fremont	theparanormaldetectives. com
Carolina Haunted And Supernatural Enlightenment Research Soc	Jacksonville	chasersnc.com
Orbs of Light Paranormal Research and Investigations	Jacksonville	ghostseeking.webs.com
South East Paranormal Investigators Association (SEPIA)	Jacksonville	sepianc.com
G.H.O.S.T.S. of Raleigh	Raleigh	ghostsofraleigh.com
NC H.A.G.S	Raleigh	nchags.org
Southeastern Paranormal Society	Salisbury	separanormal.com
Wilmington Paranormal Research	Wilmington	facebook.com/wilmingtonparanormalresearch
Autumn Moon Paranormal	Winston Salem	autumnmoonparanormal. net
True Time Paranormal Investigations	Bismarck	truetimeparanormal.webs. com

OHIO		
Akron Paranormal Investigations	Akron	akronparanormalinvestiga-tions.weebly.com
Ohio White Noise Paranormal Society	Camden	facebook.com/pages/ Ohio-White-Noise-Paranormal-Society/ 209571295863996
Anomalous Research Cincinnati	Cincinnati	arcohio.com
C-Bus Paranormal	Columbus	cbusparanormal.com
Ohio Truth Hunters	Cuyahoga Falls	ohiotruthhunters.org
Paranormal Scientific Investigators	Greenfield	orgsites.com/oh/psi/
Massillon Ghost Hunters Society	Massillon	massillonghosthunters. com#sthash.OfkSN6Rx. dpuf
Steel Valley Paranormal	Mineral Ridge	steelvalleyparanormal.org
North Canton Paranormal Detectives	North Canton	ncpdohio.com
Lone Wolf Paranormal Investigation	Northfield Ctr.	lonewolfparanormal. jimdo.com
Paranormal Spirit Encounter Investigations	Perrysburg	parasei.com
EctoVision Paranormal	Ravenna	evparanormal.com/

T-Town Paranormal Investigations	Toledo	ttownpi.com
ParaVizionz Paranormal	Trenton	paravizionz.com
The Haunted Housewives	Willoughby	hauntedhousewives.com

OKLAHOMA		
Gateway Paranormal Research & Investigation	Oklahoma City	gatewayparanormal.net
Red Dirt Paranormal of Oklahoma	Tulsa	rdpofoklahoma.com

OREGON		
Iservethelight.com	Portland	iservethelight.com
North Oregon Paranormal Investigators	Portland	northoregonpi.com

PENNSYLVANIA		
LightSeekers Paranormal Resolutions	Brookhaven	lprpa.net
Cressona Paranormal	Cressona	northernboundsouls.com
Paranormal Research Enthusiasts of Pennsylvania	Dillsburg	prepcrewonline.org

Complete Paranormal Services	Hershey	cpsparanormal.com
Paranormal Society of Indiana University of Pennsylvania	Indiana	psiup.com
Paranormal 215	Jenkintown	paranormal215.com
F.A.I.T.H. Paranormal	Lancaster	faithparanormal.com
Black Moon Paranormal Society of PA	Middletown	blackmoonparanormalsociety.com
New York Pennsylvania Paranormal Society	Montrose	freewebs.com/ xxghostsandspiritsxx/
ALKO PSI Paranormal Site Investigators	Natrona Heights	alkopsi.com
Southeast Paranormal Investigation and Research Team of PA	Philadelphia	spirtofpa.com
Point Paranormal Investigations	Pittsburgh	pointparanormalpgh.com
Steel Town Paranormal	Pittsburgh	steeltownparanormal.com
The Berks Mont Project	Pottstown	berksmontproject.org
Paranormal Research Organization Of Freedom	Proof	wtv-zone.com/hoko/ Proof.html

The Pennsylvania Paranormal Association	Scranton	theppa.net
Soul Patrol Paranormal	So. Williamsport	soulpatrolparanormalin-vestigations.weebly.com/
DeadLine Paranormal	Wilkes-Barre	deadlineparanormal.com
York County Paranormal Investigations	York	yorkcountyparanormalin-vestigation.webs.com

RHODE ISLAND		
The Rhode Island Paranormal Research Group and Society	Coventry	triprg.com
DLH Paranormal Investigations	Lincoln	dlhparanormal.com

SOUTH CAROLINA		
Carolina Society for Paranormal Research and Investigation	Anderson	carolinaspri.net
Paranormal Unexplained Metaphysics Association of the Caroli	Lexington	pumase.com
Southern Atlantic Paranormal	Lexington	southernatlanticparanormal.org
Paranormal Research Org. of the Southeast	Ninety Six	paranormal-research-org-se.webs.com

TENNESSEE		
Sycamore Valley Paranormal Research	Ashland City	sycamorevalleyparanormalresearch.webs.com
Paranormal Research Ghost Investigations	Chattanooga	prgi4ghosts.com
The Paranormal Analyst	Clarksville	TheParanormalAnalyst.com
Dead Time Paranormal Research/DTPR	Lafollette	deadtimeparanormalresearch.weebly.com
FAMILY HAUNTS	Lewisburg	familyhaunts.com
East Tennessee Ghost Seekers	Maryville	easttnghostseekers.com
Memphis – Midsouth Ghost Hunters	Memphis	memphisghosthunters.com
Nashville Ghost and Paranormal Investigators	Nashville	ngpionline.com
North American Paranormal Research Team	Seymour	naprt.com
Tennessee Paranormal Society	Sparta	tennesseeparanormalsociety.com

TEXAS		
Greater Arlington Paranormal Society	Arlington	arlingtonparanormal.com
24 Hour Paranormal	Dallas	24hourparanormal.com
ASUP INC. – DFW Paranormal Research Group	Dallas	asupinc.org

D&S Paranormal Crew	Dallas	dsparanormalcrew.wix.com/dsparanormalcrew
Texoma Paranormal Investigators Network	Gordonville	texasparanormalinvestigatorsnetwork.com
Got Haunts? Paranormal	Round Rock	gothauntsparanormal.net
San Antonio Paranormal and Occult Research Society	San Antonio	neferuaten11.wix.com/sapors
Paranormal Organization of South Texas	Victoria	parasouthtx.com

UTAH		
Utah Ghost Society	Brigham	utahghostsociety.com
W.I.S.P.S. - Demonology	Provo	wisps.org
Oquirrh Mountain Paranormal Investigators	Riverton	oquirrhmountainpi.com
4 Element Paranormal Investigations	Salt Lake City	4-element-paranormal.com/

VIRGINIA		
Southern Highlands Paranormal Investigations Group	Bristol	shpig.org
3:33am Paranormal Research	Chester Gap	333amparanormalresearch.com

Fredericksburg Paranormal Research & Investigations	Fredericksburg	fred-pri.com
Virginia Investigators of the Paranormal LLC	Fredericksburg	paranormalvip.org
Grave Concerns Paranormal	New Hope	gcparanormal.com
Old Dominion Ghost Hunters	Norfolk	odughosthunters.com
Black Diamond Paranormal Society	North Tazewell	blackdiamondps.org
East Coast Ghosts – Paranormal Research Group	Reston	eastcoastghosts.com
Research Society Virginia Paranormal	Salem	rsvparanormal.com
Spirit Chasers	Sterling	spirit-chasers.com
Tidewater Paranormal	Virginia Beach	tidewaterparanormal. yolasite.com
Virginia Paranormal Research Society	Warrenton	virginiaparanormalre- searchsociety.com

WASHINGTON		
Washington State Paranormal Investigations and Research	Issaquah	wspir.com
White Light Paranormal Insight	Portland	whitelightparanormalin- sight.com

(AGHOST) Advanced Ghost Hunters of Seattle – Tacoma	Seattle	aghost.org
Washington Psychic and Paranormal Group	Silverdale	meetup.com/ washington-psychic-and-paranormal-group

WEST VIRGINIA		
West Virginia Paranormal Research Society	Morgantown	wvprs.webs.com

WISCONSIN		
Midwestern Paranormal Investigative Network	Appleton	mpinetwork. wordpress.com
Paradigm Shift Paranormal Investigations	Fond du Lac	paradigmshiftparanormal-investigations.com
PsyCon	Fond du Lac	rebeccafoster.co
Green Bay Area Paranormal Society	Green Bay	greenbayareaparanormal-society.weebly.com
Milwaukee Independent Paranormal	Milwaukee	paulgasper.wix.com/ mkeindieparanormal
paranormal investigators of Milwaukee	Milwaukee	paranormalmilwaukee.com

Fox Valley Ghost Hunters	New London	fvghosthunters.com
Wisconsin Investigating Paranormal	Portage	hwpi.webs.com
Tri County Paranormal Group	Wausau	tricountyparanormal-group.com

Bibliography

~~~~~~~

Alleman, (Pierce) Tillie, *At Gettysburg, or What a Girl Saw and Heard of the Battle* (1888, reprinted 1994).

Corbitt, R. M.; *History of Jones County, Iowa, Past and Present;* S. J. Clarke Publishing Co., Chicago, 1910.

Gerrish, Theo. *A Private's Reminiscences of the Civil War* (1882).

Ott, Thomas. "A Grave Position For Mentor To Be In, It's Not Certain Stone Really Marks Remains." *Cleveland Plain Dealer*, December 8, 1998, pg 1B.

Zacher, Susan M. "Sauck's (Sachs) Covered Bridge" (1980).